# Troubleshooting your PC printer

# OTHER TITLES BY THE SAME AUTHOR

# Troubleshooting your PC printer

by

Ian Sinclair

BERNARD BABANI (publishing) LTD
THE GRAMPIANS
SHEPHERDS BUSH ROAD
LONDON W6 7NF
ENGLAND

# PLEASE NOTE

Although every care has been taken with the production of this book to ensure that any projects, designs, modifications and/or programs, etc., contained herewith, operate in a correct and safe manner and also that any components specified are normally available in Great Britain, the Publishers and Author(s) do not accept responsibility in any way for the failure (including fault in design) of any project, design, modification or program to work correctly or to cause damage to any equipment that it may be connected to or used in conjunction with, or in respect of any other damage or injury that may be so caused, nor do the Publishers accept responsibility in any way for the failure to obtain specified components.

Notice is also given that if equipment that is still under warranty is modified in any way or used or connected with home-built equipment then that warranty may be void.

© 1998 BERNARD BABANI (publishing) LTD

First Published –July 1998


British Library Cataloguing in Publication Data:

A catalogue record for this book is available from the British Library

ISBN 0 85934 451 7


Cover Design by Gregor Arthur
Cover Illustration by Adam Willis
Printed and Bound in Great Britain by Cox & Wyman Ltd., Reading

# PREFACE

PC printers are often bought separately from the PC, and though virtually any printer will work with any PC computer, it is quite another matter to buy a printer that is best suited to the type of work you intend it for. A printer is mechanically complicated, and is driven by software, so that there are a lot of things that can go wrong, proving the truth of the old maxim that anything that can go wrong will do so at some time.

Most printer users, particularly new users, will always suspect the hardware when something goes wrong, but the cause is quite often the software, the printer driver. In this book, both the hardware and the software are considered, and we look at what can go wrong, the symptoms that you see, and what to do about it. One important point to remember is that both the hardware and the software are subject to constant revision, so that some potential flaws are eliminated but others can appear.

This is therefore not a long list of symptoms and causes, because these change as fast as versions of your software and hardware. The aim of this book is to show you how to find the cause of faults and where to look for detailed information; it's like providing seeds rather than food.

There are some faults that can be remedied with very little skill or knowledge, some that need a little more understanding, some that need expert attention. The hardware of the printer itself is not necessarily complicated, but there are no-go areas such as the optical system of a laser printer that you should leave strictly to the professionals unless you have had some experience in servicing copiers or allied equipment. You can, however, work on a dot-matrix printer without any precautions other than disconnecting it from the computer and from the mains. Inkjet servicing is not encouraged by the manufacturers, but some simple cleaning and adjustment is not difficult to carry out.

Software tips are mainly concerned with Windows 95 and Windows 98, since this is the software that every modern PC machine is certain to use, though some older machines will still be using Windows 3.1 or 3.11. There are some programs that are notorious for causing problems, but they are likely to be out of use, or rewritten by the time this book appears.

My hope is that the use of this book will for some readers at least, minimise the impact of that moment the printer stays silent, produces gibberish, or decides to produce spectacularly stained paper.

One potential source of problems has been omitted. This book does not deal with networked printers, because the problems that can be encountered using networks would require a book to themselves of many times this size. Many networking problems require the attention of an expert and considerable help from the supplier of the network, whereas this book has been directed at the owner-user of the printer, and particularly applies to one-off desktop machines.

The book is not aimed at any particular age or occupation of printer user, and I should remind young readers that notes on making repairs to the inside of a printer assume that you know the elements of electrical safety. If in doubt, always work under supervision, and never on laser printers.

No single book can be a substitute for experience in this respect, and I urge each reader to subscribe to a good PC magazine and to keep a paper file of the hints that appear each month. This allows you to build up a collection of useful tips that will help when you encounter an elusive problem. The Internet is also an amazing route to all the collective wisdom that exists on printers and their quirks.

The points that are covered in this book are intended to be relevant to printers old and new, with particular reference to machines that by now will be well out of guarantee time.

Ian Sinclair

Spring 1998

# ABOUT THE AUTHOR

Ian Sinclair was born in 1932 in Tayport, Fife, and graduated from the University of St. Andrews in 1956. In that year, he joined the English Electric Valve Co. in Chelmsford, Essex, to work on the design of specialised cathode-ray tubes, and later on small transmitting valves and TV transmitting tubes.

In 1966, he became an assistant lecturer at Hornchurch Technical College, and in 1967 joined the staff of Braintree College of F.E. as a lecturer. His first book, "Understanding Electronic Components" was published in 1972, and he has been writing ever since, particularly for the novice in Electronics or Computing. The interest in computing arose after seeing a Tandy TRS80 in San Francisco in 1977, and of his 180 published books, about half have been on computing topics, starting with a guide to Microsoft Basic on the TRS80 in 1979.

He left teaching in 1984 to concentrate entirely on writing, and has also gained experience in computer typesetting, particularly for mathematical texts. He has recently visited Seattle to see Microsoft at work, and to remind them that he has been using Microsoft products longer than most Microsoft employees can remember.

# ACKNOWLEDGEMENTS

I would like to thank the staff of Text 100 Ltd. for providing the Windows 95 software which is so frequently mentioned in the course of this book. I would also like to thank Mike Eyres of Asset Recovery for his efforts to find me an Olivetti JP170S printer. I also acknowledge the useful information held on the Web sites of printer manufacturers and the comments made by printer users.

# TRADEMARKS

Microsoft, MS-DOS, Windows, Windows 95 and NT are either registered trademarks or trademarks of Microsoft Corporation.

All other brand and product names used in this book are recognised as trademarks, or registered trademarks, of their respective companies.

x

# CONTENTS

# 1 Printer types

## Evolution

A printer is by now such an essential part of a computer system that you tend to forget that it is not always part of a computer package. Unlike the monitor, the printer is often bought separately, so that your choice of printer is important, since it may outlive several computers (in the sense that the computers are replaced by newer devices but the printer is not). In addition, it is reasonable nowadays for all but the smallest system to use more than one printer or to share the use of a printer among several computers.

Output on paper is referred to as *hard copy*, and this hard copy is essential if the computer is to be of any use in business applications. For word processing uses, it's not enough just to have a printer, you need a printer with a high quality output whose characters are as clear as those of a first-class electric typewriter. For desktop publishing purposes you will need a laser type of printer. On the other hand, if your needs are simple, you need not seek the most expensive printer types, and you can get remarkably good value for money with printers that are slightly out of date or out of fashion. Given that the use of a printer is a priority for the serious computer user, what sort of printers are available?

The answer is any type that comes with a parallel interface, which means virtually any printer currently on sale, though some bargain offers may have the alternative serial type of interface. The parallel type of interface, also called a *Centronics* interface, means that each of the eight electrical signals that are used when you print a character will be sent to the printer over a separate wire, so that when control wires are also added, the cable between the computer and the printer contains a large number of wires, and is usually either a thick cable or a ribbon type. Modern cables of the

# Troubleshooting your PC printer

type called *bi-directional* also provide additional wires for signals to be sent from the printer to the computer.

This data cable system is simple and easy to set up; you simply plug in the cable and start printing. This is due to the standardisation, many years ago, of the connections by the printer manufacturer Centronics. The only disadvantage of this system is that parallel printer leads from computers cannot be much longer than 2 metres, and most printer cables are only 1 m long. This is needed to avoid interference between the signals.

- The alternative is a networked printer, with one printer close to a computer and the other computers connected to the network, or a serial printer that can use a cable that can be (typically) up to 50 m long. Several makes of machines allow for both serial and parallel input, because the Apple computers use serial printer output.

Only a few portable computers nowadays omit a Centronics port, and it's best to avoid such machines unless the price is irresistible or if you can network the machine to your desktop computer and use its printer. Printers that are used with small computers are virtually all either impact dot matrix, inkjet, or laser printers.

## Impact dot-matrix

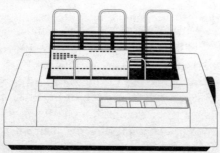

Of these, the impact dot matrix type is still the most common. A dot matrix printer creates each character out of a set of dots, and when you look at the print closely, you can see the dot structure. Inkjet and laser printers also create character shapes from dots of ink, but the name dot matrix is reserved for the older *impact* type in which the paper is marked by the impact of a metal needle on an inked ribbon or carbon ribbon which hits the paper.

The older type of dot matrix printer used a print-head that contained 9 wires or needles in a vertical line. This 9-pin, or 9-wire, printer type is still manufactured in large quantities, and some are sold at very high prices because of their particularly robust construction or high speed printing or both. Some makes are renowned for a very long working life, and they have advantages (such as use with multi-part stationery) that keeps them selling.

A later trend was to the use of 24-pin printers. By using two slightly staggered vertical rows of 12 pins each, these printers can print at a high speed and with excellent quality with none of the dotty appearance that has been associated with dot-matrix printers in the past. The noise level of such printers is usually higher than that of the 9-pin types, and ribbon life is shorter since so many more pins are striking the ribbon. Each pin is of a smaller diameter than a human hair. Some 48-pin models were sold at one time, but disappeared again.

There is a huge range of manufacturers, but most printers are set up so as to emulate either the IBM range of Proprinters or the Epson types — most 24-pin printers will provide emulation of the Epson LQ type. Emulation means that a printer will accept the signals for another model, so that the software, the printer driver, for that other model can be used.

- Some emulations are not satisfactory, because they can lead to a 24-pin printer being used to emulate a 9-pin type, so that the superior quality that the 24-pin type can provide for graphics use is not being utilised.

## Troubleshooting your PC printer

Paper handling on dot matrix printers is usually biased to tractor feed. The printer roller (*platen*) is provided with a pair of toothed wheels which engage in perforations in the paper and ensure that the paper can be kept precisely in place. The paper is rolled or folded (fan-fold paper) into a pack, with perforations to allow the sheets to be separated and the perforated edges to be removed easily. The alternative is to use single sheets fed by hand, and if this is done there is usually some method of ensuring that the sheet is rolled to the correct position before printing starts (this is often done automatically when the paper is inserted).

Automatic feeders for single sheets can be bought for some dot matrix printers, but they are often ridiculously expensive when you consider that cheap inkjet printers come with sheet feeders built in, and for the same price as some add-on feeders for dot matrix printers.

Colour printing with dot-matrix printers has been possible for some considerable time, but the colour printers of this type had a short selling life because of the competition from colour inkjet machines, see later.

### Inkjet machines

The inkjet printer, which operates by squirting tiny jets of ink at paper from a set of miniature syringes, can be a close second in quality to the laser printer. The bubblejet technology, developed by Canon and Hewlett-Packard, has been widely adopted to make printers of remarkable quality and reliability at comparatively low prices. The mechanisms (*print engines*) provided by these manufacturers have been used by other makers, so that a vast number of inkjet makes and models are in reality re-badged versions of the Canon or Hewlett-Packard engines.

The accepted story is that this technology originated when a technician laid a hot soldering iron on a hypodermic needle and noticed that it caused a drop of liquid to be ejected. The principle is to use a head consisting of fine tubes (of a diameter narrower than a human hair) each provided with a miniature heater wire. One end of each tube is fed with ink, and passing current through the heater for a tube will expel a tiny drop of ink, so that by driving these heater wires with the same form of signals as a dot-matrix impact printer, the ink can be deposited in the same character patterns.

A disadvantage of this type is that the tubes clog, and though a minor blockage can be cleared by using software that forces ink more vigorously through the tubes, the heads have to be replaced at intervals. Some manufacturers make the ink cartridge and print head in one unit, so that when you fit a new cartridge you are also renewing the (expensive) print head. Others make the head and cartridge as separate units, so that several cartridges of ink can be used before the head has to be renewed.

- If you want to be able to print, for example, a hundred pages in one session, you may find that a laser printer would be a better choice, because print quality on inkjet machines can vary in quality over a printing session, particularly when you are using draft printing mode.

A more recent development is the piezo-inkjet printer developed by Epson. The principle here is that part of the jet path is through a piezoelectric crystal (one that deforms when a voltage is applied to it), and when a voltage pulse is applied to the crystal it contracts, forcing ink from the jet. At the time of writing, no other manufacturer has taken up the principle, and the Epson mechanisms are not sold under any other name. The claimed advantage is that the printing head is permanent, and only the ink cartridges need to be changed, but this has not been my own experience.

Initially, all inkjet printers were monochrome, but manufacturers soon realised that it was just as easy to print in colour, and it is now very difficult to find a monochrome inkjet printer. If your main needs are for monochrome printing this can be a drawback, because though all inkjet printers use both a black and a colour cartridge, some cannot be used for monochrome unless the colour cartridge is present. Some older types used only a colour cartridge, and could not print a true black, only a muddy brown.

- Ink cartridges and ink/head combinations are expensive, and several firms offer recycled ink cartridges at a considerably lower price than the original, and there are also re-inking kits available. The topic of re-inking is deal with in more detail in Chapter 7.

Bubble-jet types are remarkably silent, considerably quieter than some laser types (many of which have a noisy cooling fan). The piezo-electric type, by contrast, is as noisy as an impact dot-matrix printer. The speed of printing is not as high as that of the faster laser type, but for many applications this is of little importance, and ability to print in colour may be the feature that tips the balance of choice for you.

## Laser printers

The ultimate in print quality at the present time can be provided by the laser type of printer, which also includes variants such as LED bar printers and LCD-mask printers, now very rare. These are fast and silent in action. The 'classic' laser types are page printers, meaning that the printer has to store a complete page of information in its memory before it can print the page. When elaborate graphics are used, this can require a large amount of memory, and some laser printers will require 2 Mbyte or more of memory to work satisfactorily with DTP material.

• This has led to the introduction of Windows (or GDI) printers, which use some of the computer's memory for this purpose. This memory has to be allocated by Windows, so that these printers cannot be used by DOS programs, hence the name. A Windows laser printer can be less costly than the conventional type, but you need to have a computer with a reasonable amount of RAM, which nowadays means 32 Mbyte or more. Older GDI printers were designed for Windows 3.1 and some will not work correctly under Windows 95.

• LED and LCD bar types are line printers, not page printers, and because they need store only a line at a time, they require very little memory. A notable modern example of this type is the Oki 4W. Minolta also manufacture a range of printers of this type. See later for more information.

# Troubleshooting your PC printer

- The quoted speed of most laser printers refers to repeated copies of a single page and does **not** refer to normal printing, which can be considerably slower because each page has to be converted into its set of codes in the memory. All quoted printing speeds for printers of any kind tend to be optimistic.

The laser printer uses a drum of material which is electrically charged by an electrical discharge (a *corona*) through air. Any electrically charged object will attract small particles to it, and the purpose of charging the drum is to make it possible for finely-powdered ink (called *toner*) to stick to the drum. The principle of the printer is to make the drum conductive in selected parts, and this happens when the material is made conductive by being struck by a laser beam. The beam is switched on and off and its direction is controlled by the pattern of signals held in the memory of the printer, and enough memory must be present to store information for a complete page.

Rolling a sheet of paper over the drum will now pass the toner to the paper. This leaves the toner only very faintly adhering to the paper, and it needs to be fixed permanently into place by passing the paper between hot rollers which melt the toner into the paper, giving the glossy appearance that is the mark of a good laser printer.

- This heating also merges the dots of toner, so that the print from a laser printer, seen under a magnifying glass, show none of the separate dots that can be seen when a dot-matrix or inkjet printer has been used. In addition, the melting of the toner sinks the toner into the paper rather than allowing it to spread sideways, which is another fault that can be seen when inkjet printer is examined through a magnifier.

- You should not open up a conventional laser printer unless you have experience with copiers or other laser-fitted equipment, and you must never under any circumstances apply power to a laser mechanism when the casing has been removed. There are references in this book to faults that are caused by misalignment of the revolving mirror that is part of a laser engine, but this should not be taken as an indication that you can adjust this for yourself.

The laser printer is not the universal answer to printing requirements, because though the cost of buying a laser printer has dropped dramatically since the early days, the price of maintaining such a printer is still high, though not as high as some ink-jet models that need expensive coated paper and short-lived ink cartridges. The consumables are costly, particularly toner (powdered ink), and when more extensive servicing is required the chemicals that are involved are toxic and expensive.

## Daisywheel printers

A daisywheel printer is old technology, and it works by using a set of cast metal or plastic shapes of each letter and symbol set on stalks on a wheel, the daisywheel of the name. As the wheel is moved back and forward across the paper, the wheel is spun to position each letter and a miniature hammer is fired by an electromagnet when the required character is in place. As for dot-matrix printers, there is an ink or carbon (usually carbon) ribbon placed between the daisywheel and the paper.

Daisywheel printers were once very popular because they can produce much better-looking typed copy than the early 9-pin dot-matrix printers. Their disadvantages include very slow speed and a very high noise level, a character set that is limited to what is provided on the printwheel, and the total inability to print graphics.

An alternative to the daisywheel at one time was the electronic typewriter. Some of these, notably the IBM types, could have an interface added so that the typewriter could be connected to the PC so as to be used as a printer. This did not interfere with its ability to be used as an ordinary typewriter.

Since both daisywheel printers and typewriters are impact printers they can be used with carbon paper to make copies. Daisywheel printers can usually print on continuous paper as well as on single sheets or labels, but adapted typewriters are usually limited to single sheets and labels with the paper manually fed.

The printing performance of either type is usually quoted in terms of characters per second (cps).

These forms of printers have been almost entirely replaced by 24-pin dot matrix and laser types for most business applications, though they can still be found (and heard) in some smaller offices. Their lack of versatility has been the deciding factor in their decline because no graphics can be printed. Software fonts, such as Windows TrueType, cannot be used, and any change of font can be done only by changing the print-wheel. The other side of all this is that daisywheel printers can now be bought for much less than the cost of a portable typewriter. Unless you need only text and can buy very cheaply, avoid this type of printer.

## Plotters

Another way of producing paper output, mainly for line drawings, is the pen plotter, which uses a set of up to 8 miniature ball pens moving over a sheet of paper. The top-quality plotters (such as the Hewlett-Packard range) are expensive, but ideally suited to CAD work. Lower-cost plotters are available, but mostly for work on small paper sizes compared to the A3 which is a standard for graphics work. Plotters are ideally suited to producing line drawings in colour because each pen can be of a different colour. The action is very slow, and a detailed drawing may take hours to produce.

## Jurassic printers

Printers were used with computers long before we had desktop machines, and for the sake of completing the story, we should take a brief look at some of the older systems. One of the oldest (still in use) is the line printer which is still the most common way of printing huge numbers of documents at high speed. These use a rotating cylinder or a chain containing all of the printable characters in metal type form.

The rotating cylinder type has a complete set of characters (in order of most frequent use) around the cylinder in each column position. As the cylinder rotates, hammers move the paper against the ribbon and the cylinder when the character to print is at the right position. The rotating chain type also contains the character set repeated several times and the paper is hammered against the ribbon and the chain when the character to be printed is at the correct position.

A belt printer uses type stalks, like a daisywheel printer but with the stalks mounted on a flexible belt. Because the belt is flexible, the hammer action moves the type stalks on to the ribbon and paper. The printing speed of all these older types of printers is very high, though not as high as some modern laser types, and never as high as the speed of a conventional printing press.

Other old printer types include variations on the dot-matrix theme, such as thermal printers that use heat-sensitive paper and make marks by using hot needles. These are still found on older fax machines. Though printing is silent, the paper is costly and the print fades badly after a year or so. Another variation that has definitely disappeared is the electrostatic printer. This used aluminium-clad black paper, with needles in a matrix pattern removing dots of aluminium by sparking.

# Troubleshooting your PC printer

This technology was used in the Sinclair Spectrum printer (and if you still have one, try it on the Antiques Road Show in a few years time).

## Others

There are some printers that are not used for text, do not fit into any convenient category and which are not easy to find, but which are ideal for specific purposes. The most important of these at the time of writing is the dye-sublimation printer. This uses coloured dyes that are vaporised before mixing, so that true colour mixing as distinct from using a set of dots of different colours, can be achieved. The action deposits dry ink, and demands the use of high-quality glossy paper. Another type of colour technology is wax-ribbon, which uses ribbons as the source of coloured dyes which are transparent enough to allow colour mixing on glossy paper.

These specialised printer types are used for photographic quality reproduction, and though the results can be excellent the cost of the paper and the other consumables is high, and the time to make a print can be very long, twenty minutes or more for a high-resolution large colour print.

# 2 Buying a printer

## What are your needs?

If you are about to buy your first printer, or to replace a printer that you have used for many years you need to give a lot of care to finding one that will suit your needs for a considerable time to come. First of all, you have to think long and hard about just what your needs are.

How **much** printing do you do? Will your printer be busy for three or more hours each day, or is it lightly used printing a few letters each Sunday morning? If your printer is intensively used it needs to be a robust type intended for office use rather than a light and delicate model intended only for occasional use. Some printers that seem quite fragile are, in fact, tough as the proverbial old boot and capable of a very long active life, others are so delicate that you would hesitate to drop a typewriter cover over them. One particularly vulnerable point is the paper feed guide, which is often a piece of thin plastic fitting into a plastic holder. This will usually snap off if subjected to any force.

Another consideration that is tied up with how much printing you do is whether or not you have any business uses. If your printer is used for business purposes and is claimed as a legitimate cost against tax, you may feel that you can afford a more professional grade of printer than would be possible if you had only hobby use in mind.

In addition to quantity of printing you have to consider **quality** of printing. If your only use of a printer is to get paper copy of information from the Internet, for example, the quality of printing is not the most important factor to you, and the type of printer referred to as a draft printer is perfectly suitable (or the draft mode of some inkjet printers).

By contrast, if you want to use a printer to obtain the best possible reproduction of photographs in digital form (from a scanner or from a digital camera) you will need a colour printer with very high resolution. This might indicate an inkjet used with very expensive coated paper, or a different type of printer that is intended just for this purpose, such as a dye-sublimation printer.

- The resolution of a printer is quoted in terms of the number of dots per inch it can produce, and the figures are often given separately for horizontal and vertical directions. For example, a resolution of $600 \times 600$ means that 600 dots per inch can be achieved in both directions, but $600 \times 300$ means that the resolution in the horizontal direction is twice as good as in the vertical direction.

Between the extremes of quality, there is a large range of requirements. You may want to produce print that looks as good as print in a book, which will for many users rule out an impact dot-matrix printer. If you are printing camera-ready sheets, meaning book pages that a commercial printer will prepare for lithography by photographing the pages, you need a laser printer that will produce crisp clean copy with no trace of dots or streaks. The number of pages you are likely to be printing will enforce the use of copy paper at around £3.00 per pack of 500 sheets (one ream), and you certainly cannot contemplate the use of an inkjet using paper at more than 50p per sheet.

If you print the parish magazine, or you want to type a thesis, and particularly if you want colour illustrations, there is no realistic low-cost alternative to an inkjet machine, but you need to choose with considerable care. All inkjet machines can make use of expensive coated paper to advantage, but some machines are very much better than others at producing good results on ordinary (laser-grade) copy paper. Some inkjet printers seem to be much more sensitive to the quality of paper than others.

## Printer price

Printer prices vary enormously, and price is not necessarily related to value. You cannot ensure that you will be satisfied with a printer that cost a lot, nor can you be assured that you have a bargain if you spent very little. As for all computer-related purchases, a few weeks spent studying the advertisements in the magazines will be well rewarded. Do not assume that a laser printer that is well suited to your needs will be more expensive than an inkjet.

A new model of printer can be very attractive, particularly if the price is right, but if anything goes wrong it can prove very irritating and costly in terms of telephone calls and return carriage. When a printer has been on sale for some time, a knowledge base will have built up so that its weaknesses are well-known, and advice is available, particularly on the Internet — try the Deja News site for information that advertisers and manufacturers are not likely to provide. The Deja News site is at:

**http://w2.dejanews.com/**

and you can often find either notes on printer problems or references to web sites that provide answers to FAQ (frequently asked questions).

You will find that when a printer is about to be replaced by a new model (or has already been replaced) there will be bargain offers of the older stock. Do not assume that these prices are the lowest you will get, because the larger suppliers usually do not keep stocks if they can avoid it, and you may well find lower prices from smaller suppliers later.

- Remember that printers that have low price-tags attached might have high running costs. This is another instance of the value of checking for comments on the Web.

# Troubleshooting your PC printer

At the time of writing, prices were changing rapidly, and there is an amazing range of prices for each type of printer. This price range reflects the expected type of use. For example, taking impact dot-matrix printers, you can buy the Epson LX-300 for around £100, but the Epson DFX-8000 costs closer to £2,000. Both are 9-pin machines, and the price difference reflects the fact that the DFX-8000 is an office machine that has a wide (132 columns) carriage and is intended to work all day every day for many years. Considering that my old RX-80 printer is still working after some fourteen years, the lifetime of even the cheaper machines need not be short if they are appropriately used.

Inkjet machines are offered at even lower prices than impact dot-matrix types, and at the lower end of the scale, there are genuine bargains to be had. One current example is the Olivetti JP170S, which at around £90 (including VAT and carriage) is a genuine bargain with performance that is out of all proportion to its price. It's not so easy to single out bargains in the higher price range, because you will find that you are paying a lot extra for features that you might not necessarily want, such as faster printing or the ability to achieve very high resolution on costly coated paper (at up to 90p per sheet). Prices up to £1,500 indicate just how costly these features can be.

Laser printers show a similar scatter, with the lowest prices attached to models that use Windows memory, print comparatively slowly, and print in monochrome. The price range goes from about £180 for a Windows monochrome type to more than £4,000 for a fast colour printer.

## Cost of consumables

You cannot separate the cost of a printer from the cost of the consumables, such as paper and ink, that you need to keep it running. If your volume of printing is small, these costs may be negligible as far as you are concerned, but for large-volume work the cost of the consumables can easily exceed the cost of a cheap printer over a year.

The impact dot-matrix type of printer has the lowest running costs, because it can print happily on any type of paper. In addition, some models have a very long ribbon life, ribbons are not costly and can be re-inked. The 9-pin types are among the most economical, particularly the types which use a ribbon cartridge that extends for the full width of the carriage and does not move with the print head.

Some 24-pin types, by contrast, have a short ribbon life, and you can always expect the life to be short if the ribbon is held in a small cartridge that moves with the print head. Even re-inking may not be an answer to ribbon costs for these cartridges because the ribbon becomes too badly worn to be useable, and will eventually jam.

Inkjet printers have almost uniformly high ink costs, and the cost of paper will depend on your requirements. Some makes use black cartridges of reasonable size that will see out almost 1,000 sheets of text, others will be hard pressed to last for half that amount. Colour cartridges can have a frighteningly short life if you print large colour pictures with areas of solid colour. Most manufacturers will frown on refilling, but for most users this is what makes the inkjet an economical proposition. One inkjet model, the Olivetti JP170S, is sold on the basis that its cartridge can easily be refilled (but the handbook insists that you should not do so, and gives no instructions).

The cost of paper is the more serious problem. Any inkjet ought to be able to provide clear text of good appearance on ordinary copier grade paper at around £3.00 per ream (500 sheets). Such paper comes in a pack that carries an arrow to show which is the better side for printing, and you should observe this, though the difference in results is often not easy to tell. If, however, you bought the inkjet to print at very high resolution (more than 700 dots per inch) and

# Troubleshooting your PC printer

particularly if you bought it in the hope of making enlarged prints of scanned photographs, then you simply have to be prepared to spend out on suitable paper. The same, more obviously, applies to printing iron-on transfers and preparing overhead projector (OHP) transparencies.

Laser printers of any price can use low-cost paper of copier grade, and can produce monochrome text and graphics print of excellent quality, suitable for camera-ready typesetting copy to a printing firm. Not all will handle graphics well, and only the most expensive machines will work with colour. In general, monochrome line graphics are no problem, but any pictures with large black areas may be poorly handled by some laser printers. This is something that you can find only by using a test page.

Paper is the most consumed item, and all laser printers can use, as might be expected, the photocopier grade of paper which is only slightly more expensive than plain paper. The reason for the additional cost is because of the way that the toner is deposited on to the paper. The paper should consist of fibres which are all aligned along the longer axis of the paper, making the paper behave more uniformly when subject to electric charges (and discharges). It also allows the paper to feed through the machine with less tendency to curl.

In addition, since the toner is fixed to the paper by fairly intense heating, the paper must not darken or curl when it is heated. These requirements make the paper more expensive to produce, though some shopping around can reveal better prices than can be obtained from local suppliers. Try Staples or Viking Direct if you cannot obtain low-cost paper locally — and look at their catalogues also when you want other consumables like toner.

Whatever is claimed by manufacturers, the use of very heavy (more than 90 grams per square metre) and expensively finished paper is not usually justifiable for laser printers. Such paper will often feed badly, forming ridges, and will allow toner to smear. Very heavy paper will stick in the printer or cause loud protests from the rollers. Lighter and more absorbent papers usually produce better results — try cheap grades first and always try a sample before you buy several hundred packs.

The main cost for a laser printer is of toner and drum. Some machines, notably the Hewlett-Packard LaserJets, use a cartridge that contains the drum, toner, and other parts all in one pack, so that you need only remove a sealing strip and insert the cartridge to make the machine ready for printing. Others use separate drum and toner cartridges, so that a comparatively cheap (around £15–£20) toner cartridge will serve for 1,000 or more pages, and a more expensive drum cartridge is needed at longer intervals (typically 5,000 to 20,000 pages).

Toner is a fine powder which must not be allowed to spill into the atmosphere, and the print drum is constructed using a photosensitive material which must not be handled or unduly exposed to light. Some manufacturers have made the replacement of both toner and drum particularly easy for the user, for other machines the task is far from easy and better done by a maintenance mechanic. Maintenance does not simply cover the replacement of the toner and drum, it also concerns cleaning. Because of the way that electric charges attract all small particles, laser printers tend to become clogged up with fine dust, composed of stray toner and house dust in almost equal measure. Dust is, as always, an enemy of mechanical parts, so that cleaning and lubrication schedules are of considerable importance.

- Lubrication almost always uses silicone oils — mineral oils are totally forbidden on the plastics which are almost universally used for bearings on light machinery. Unless your manual shows lubrication points and a schedule for lubrication, assume that it will not be needed.

Users are often advised to start a new run of a major printing with a fresh toner supply. Though it is inadvisable to start a run when the toner is almost finished, replenishing toner is not necessary before a major piece of work. When toner has been replenished, the first set of pages may be over-inked and smudged. Following toner replenishment, always make some test copies onto absorbent paper until you are sure that the toner is flowing correctly — I have never experienced these problems with the LaserJet machine. Note that toner cannot be removed by vacuum-cleaning because it is too fine to be retained in the bag of the cleaner unless you are using a Medivac™ or Nilfisk™ type of machine. If you get toner on clothes, try to shake or brush it off. If washing is needed, use cold water and detergent. Avoid hot water at all costs because it can melt the toner into the fabric, making it impossible to remove.

You are not encouraged to refill a toner cartridge, and even if you found it possible, it is not something that you ought to try. The only opportunity for saving is the use of reconditioned drums and refilled cartridges, and that's something we shall look at in Chapter 9.

## Footprint

The footprint of a printer means the amount of desk area it needs to itself, and this is a quantity that has been dramatically reduced on modern printers. Footprint size is bound up with the paper path, and the smallest footprints are achieved by machines that take the paper from a near-vertical feeder and return it across the top of the printer. The next size up in footprint is achieved using the same style of near-vertical feeder, but with the printed paper fed on to a horizontal surface. The largest footprint is found on the older designs which take the blank sheets from a horizontal tray on one side of the printer and deliver the printed sheets on to another horizontal tray on the other side.

## Paper handling

The paper handling of a printer is very often not something that you think of when you choose a machine, but it can be important. Some machines force the paper to take a multiple S-shaped path through the printer, and the result can be to make the pages look distinctly second-hand by the time they emerge. Laser printers are particularly bad in this respect.

At the other end of the scale, some inkjet printers have a paper path that is almost straight, and even a dot-matrix machine will not bend the paper too much over its roller. A straight paper path makes it much easier to print on both sides of a sheet, because there is no curling of the paper to cause mis-feeding.

Another point is which way round the paper is fed. Most laser printers will print on the side that is facing down in the paper holder, whereas most inkjets will print on the side that is facing upwards. This is something you have to check for yourself, because it is closely related to the paper path in the printer. Dot-matrix machines, like typewriters, print on the side of paper that is away from you as you feed the paper in.

- For inkjet and laser printers that deliver printed sheets face-up, you can set the printing software to print the pages of a document in reverse order, so that the sheets will stack up with the first page on top.

Another aspect of paper handling relates to where paper is fed in and where it comes out. The older style of printer will have a horizontal paper stack on a tray, and the printed copies emerge onto another tray. More recently, the blank paper is held in a stack that is almost vertical, allowing the printer to take up less space on the desktop, but most models allow the printed copies to settle on another tray. There are a

## Troubleshooting your PC printer

few printers on which the printed copies emerge on to the desk, or even worse, over the blank pages, forcing you to stand in attendance and catch them to avoid them falling on the desk, the floor, or even going through again. Some recent laser printers are very poorly thought out in this respect.

Another very important point relates to envelopes and labels. Dot-matrix and inkjet printers can usually cope with these types, sometimes with an adjustment to a paper-thickness lever, but laser printers are more destructive. Do not try to use self-sealing envelopes in a laser printer, and place a piece of waxed paper between the sealing edges of a conventional envelope. The reason is that a laser printer contains a heater to fuse the toner, and this reaches some 200°C. This can cause glue to melt and it can seal envelopes, so that any labels that you pass through a laser printer should be clearly stated as suitable for laser printing. Ordinary labels are liable to be left inside the printer, causing problems that can be expensive to repair.

### Hidden costs

Once you have accounted for the costs of paper and ink/ribbons/toner you are entitled to feel that you know precisely how much the use of your printer will cost. There may, however, be a few hidden costs.

One is the printer cable. Most printers are not provided with a cable, and if you are replacing an older printer you may feel that you do not need one. Many modern printers, however, need a more modern type of cable, referred to as a bi-directional cable and marked *IEEE STD 1284–1984 Compliant*. This type of cable is used when the printer has no panel of switches and is controlled entirely by software in the computer. If you use the older type of printer cable, you will not get messages about the toner/ink running out, and you may not be able to control some aspects of printer use.

For many printers, the internal rollers can be clipped out for cleaning when the inevitable toner or ink spill occurs. This makes cleaning very easy, but if the rollers cannot be detached the machine may have to be returned to the factory for cleaning.

### Cartridge/ribbon life

All manufacturers quote an expected life for a ribbon, ink cartridge or toner cartridge, and you need to know how these figures relate to your use of the printer.

The usual assumptions are the use of 8.5″ × 11″ paper (US *Letter* size), with only 5% of each page inked — this corresponds to printing the letter 'E' 960 times on a page in 12-point Courier font. Using A4 paper, which is 210 × 297 mm (approximately 8.26″ × 11.7″) gives very much the same results. You may find that if your printing is confined to letters, which do not usually cover the whole printable area of a page, you will get more pages to a ribbon or cartridge than the manufacturer's figure. On the other hand, if you print a lot of graphics images on each page you can expect to get a much lower page count. Even a fairly small logo used as a letter head can use more ink that the whole of a letter page.

# 3 Connections and drivers

## Connecting up

There are two cable connections that you have to make to your printer. One is the usual mains power supply connection, and the normal pattern is to use a standard three-pin plug at one end, and a Eurosocket at the other. Note that a few printers have the main cable permanently fixed at the printer end, so that if you find that the mains supply is just a few inches further away than the cable will reach you will need to use an extension socket.

- Some printers have a fixed cable and no switch at the printer end. These will have mains power whenever the cable is plugged in, and they are usually arranged to go into a standby condition if they are not used for several minutes. You should not attempt to break the cable to connect a switch, and the best way to connect a printer of this type is by way of a socket strip fed from the auxiliary mains outlet of your computer. That way, the printer will always be switched off fully when the computer is switched off.

The other connection is the printer data cable, with the DS25 connector at the computer and the standard Centronics connection at the printer end. These cables are usually one metre long, and though you can buy longer cables, you should preferably try to locate the printer so that this cable length will be adequate.

## Connections and drivers

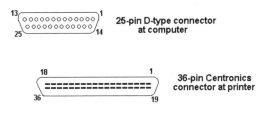

connectors viewed into pins

Some modern printers will need a bi-directional printer cable which can pass information back from the printer to the computer so that the printer can be completely driven by software. This type of software can, for example, give you an indication of how much ink remains in an inkjet cartridge. If your printer needs this type of cable, make sure that it is connected before you start the software installation for your printer.

• Note that if you have a printer that uses a bi-directional IEEE 1248 type of cable you should not attempt to connect and use a second printer that uses this type of cable. You should also avoid the use of printer switching boxes.

• Another point to watch is that the Centronics plug at the printer end of the cable must be inserted as far as it will go, and secured with the wire loops that are provided. Some printers are very easily upset if this plug is not fully home or if it is disturbed during printing.

• If you want to use two printers, connect the less-important printer to a second port (LPT2) and specify this in the printer *Properties*. This is much better than trying to use a printer switch box.

## Troubleshooting your PC printer

### Self-test

Almost every printer is capable of carrying out a self-test and printing a page without the need for any intervention by the computer. Find out from your printer manual how this is done — the usual action is to press a set of buttons simultaneously. For some printers that have no control panel on the printer itself you cannot carry out this action.

It is important to print a self-test sheet if the printer can do so. If a printer can produce a perfect copy of its test page (usually a sample of fonts and diagonal lines) then a mechanical or electrical fault is unlikely to be the cause of the problem, which is more likely to arise from incorrect settings either at the printer or at the software. Remember, for example, that when you use the Windows printer manager the printer will not necessarily start printing immediately — it may wait until a queue forms or a 'print now' instruction is issued.

- Some printer types must be disconnected from the computer before they can carry out a self-test. If your printer is one that cannot run a self-test routine at all, you may need to check it (if you cannot print from the computer) by connecting it to another computer that is set up for this model of printer.

### Port

Your printer is connected to the computer through a circuit called a *port*, and unless this port is recognised by the computer it will be impossible to print. There are two ways of connecting the computer's printer socket. One is from the main board (motherboard) of the computer, the other is by way of a small parallel port card that is inserted into one of the slots (the AT or ISA type of slot, as distinct from the smaller PCI slots that are used on modern computers). If your computer uses the motherboard type of fitting, the socket will be connected to the motherboard internally by a short length of ribbon cable. Make certain that the plug on this cable that engages into the motherboard is all the way home — these plugs are very easily loosened in the course of installing the motherboard or adding other items. If the older parallel port card method is used, make sure that the board is correctly plugged in. If you installed the card yourself, make sure that the jumper connections on the card are correctly set for LPT1 according to the documents that came with the card — see later for more information on this topic.

The usual port that is provided on all computers is labelled LPT1 (line-printer 1), and it is unusual to find that this is not installed — but it's the unusual that so often causes problems. Problems are more likely to arise if you are using a printer on another port, such as LPT2, LPT3, or LPT4.

Your port settings should appear briefly on the screen when your computer is switched on, but this display is often hidden if the video monitor has not warmed up in time or if the screen display is quickly replaced by the *Loading Windows* notice. If you have any doubts about the port setting, you need to know how to bring up the CMOS RAM display. This always requires some key or key combination to be pressed just as the computer is starting, and you may see a screen message such as:

**Press Delete key to run SETUP**

This varies from one computer to another, so that only the manual or the guide for the motherboard can be of assistance here. If you do not press the key(s) at the correct time there will be no action.

Once you can see the CMOS setup screen you can check the LPT1 settings. This will show an address, and the usual code here is either 03BCh or 0378h, and an IRQ number which is normally 7. If this appears, then the port is correctly installed as LPT1 for your printer.

## Troubleshooting your PC printer

The reason for the different address codes is that some video cards and chipsets make use of the address code 3BCh for their own purposes. These makes are Matrox, ATI mach64, TBLMB Horizon, STB2MB Powergraph, or an Aries integrated PCI system. If you have any of these, the LPT1 port will be forced to use the address of 0378h which is normally allocated to LPT1 on older machines.

• If you install other ports (for a second printer or for parallel port peripherals such as a scanner) the address for LPT2 will be 0278 and the IRQ number is 5. There may be problems in installing an LPT3 port if you have any of the video cards or chipsets noted above, because this port would normally use the 03BCh address. You should always use the Windows *Add Hardware* option of Control Panel if you put in other ports, so that conflicts can be avoided.

## Drivers

A printer is not necessarily made useful simply by connecting it up to a port. Before you can print anything much you need to install printer drivers, though there are some items that you can print using MS-DOS. I shall assume that you are more likely to be printing from Windows.

Printing from Windows is not possible until some software, the printer driver, is installed. Once the Windows driver is installed, you can print from any Windows application, such as word-processors, spreadsheets, or accounts programs. One Windows driver is all that you need for one printer, but if you use MS-DOS programs you will need a separate printer driver for each application that you use running under MS-DOS.

• Some printers nowadays provide only the Windows drivers, others provide the Windows drivers with some MS-DOS drivers as well. Do not confuse a Windows *driver* with a Windows *printer* — a Windows (or GDI) printer is a laser printer that makes use of the Windows memory of your computer instead of requiring additional memory to be installed inside the printer.

Installing your driver software for Windows can be very straightforward if your printer is a model that was in production before 1995, because this makes it almost certain that it will be listed in the Windows 95 driver set. If you are using Windows 98 you can be almost certain that any printer manufactured in and before 1998 will be listed. Even if your printer is one that Windows does not list, however, the printer manufacturer will have provided a floppy or a CD-ROM with printer drivers. If all else fails, printer drivers can be downloaded over the Internet. See appendix B for a list of manufacturer's Web sites.

**Driver installation**

Driver installation starts with being able to specify the correct printer. You need to know the name of the manufacturer and the **precise** model number of the printer. For example, if you are installing a Hewlett-Packard LaserJet IIP, it is not good enough to use the driver for the Series II — you must look for the IIP model.

With everything connected up and switched on, get to the Printers window of Windows 95 or Windows 98 in the usual way by clicking on the Start button, then on Settings and Printers. If you are using Windows 3.1 or 3.11, start in Program Manager and double-click Main. When you see control Panel, double click on this icon and then on the Printers icon. From this point on, we shall look at the Windows 95/98 installation methods.

The Windows 95/98 Printer panel includes an icon labelled *New Printer*. Double-click (or click, depending on which version you are using) on this icon to start a Wizard which will install your new printer.

## Troubleshooting your PC printer

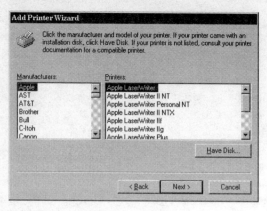

A pair of lists will appear, one on the left-hand side of printer manufacturers and another on the right hand side of models corresponding to the manufacturer whose name you have clicked. Once you have clicked manufacturer and model, you can proceed to the next part of the installation which will ask you to insert the CD-ROM (or floppies) that you used to install Windows. The driver software will be read from this source, and you can then opt to print a trial page to ensure that the driver software will operate your printer correctly.

A slightly different procedure is needed if your printer is one that is not listed. This is likely if the printer was not manufactured when Windows 95/98 was issued, and you then need to use the software that is supplied by the printer manufacturer (which you can ignore if you find the make and model listed in Windows *Add Printer* lists). In this case, you ignore the list, insert the floppy containing the drivers, and click the button marked *Have Disk*. You will then be guided by messages on the screen so that the driver is installed from the disc, and you will usually be asked to opt for printing a test page.

If you cannot find your printer listed and there is no disc of driver software (for a second-hand printer, perhaps), your options are more limited. One is to make use of a driver for a similar machine. Despite the huge number of makes and models of printers that you see advertised, there are remarkably few manufacturers of the basic mechanisms or *engines* as they are called. An inkjet or laser printer of uncertain origin, for example, will probably use an engine from either Canon or Hewlett-Packard, and most dot-matrix models use the Epson or IBM Proprinter set of codes, so that installing a driver for a model from one of these manufacturers will usually allow you to get printing, even if some actions are not supported.

Finding what **model** to emulate is not quite so easy. If there is any paperwork with your printer it may refer to another model that can be used as an *emulation* under MS-DOS, such as to the H-P DeskJet 500C or to the IBM ProPrinter. Laser printers can often make use of a driver from the Hewlett-Packard LaserJet series. If you cannot find useful information with the printer, try contacting the manufacturer, either by post or (much better) over their Internet Web site. You can also try News groups on the Net to find if anyone else in the world has experience of your problems. It's highly likely that you will get information on the printer, where to find drivers, what to watch for and how to sort out trouble.

Once you have downloaded a driver to a floppy, you can proceed with installation using the *Have Disk* option button.

## Typical problems

The typical problems that you can encounter with any type of printer are:

- The printer itself may be defective and unable to perform a self-test (if it is normally capable of a self-test).

- The printer power supply is turned off. This is always a possibility if the printer is not powered from the auxiliary power socket of the computer. Check also that the cable is connected from your printer to the computer

- The cable may be loose or defective, or of the wrong type (if a bi-directional cable is needed).

- The CMOS RAM setting for LPT1 may not be enabled.

- The printer driver may not be correctly installed, or be of the wrong type, or corrupt.

- Your printer may not be the one that is configured as the default printer in Windows.

- The printer switches are incorrectly set. The printer may be switched off-line. There may be an error message at the printer control panel. There may be a paper jam. Problems like this are common if you use a network printer that you cannot see from your desk.

- The MS-DOS application that you are using has not been configured with a driver for your particular printer. Remember that you need one driver for Windows, but you need a different printer driver for each different MS-DOS application that you use.

- For MS-DOS use only, the CONFIG.SYS or the AUTOEXEC.BAT file may contain some conflicting commands.

Mechanical problems with printers are surprisingly rare, despite the complex mechanism of many printers. One problem that can arise at times is paper jamming. Ordinary paper seldom causes any difficulties but envelopes and multi-part stationery can be troublesome, and some printers are very much better than others at handling such awkward materials.

Particular care is needed in handling sticky labels. These are normally mounted on a backing sheet, but if they become detached they can deposit their adhesive on rollers within the printer, causing problems until the rollers are removed and cleaned. If you want to use self-adhesive labels with a laser printer, make absolutely certain that the labels are laser-grade which can withstand the heat of the laser printer.

A genuine mechanical fault will usually require the printer to be returned to the manufacturer or to a service agent. Before doing this, try the printer's self-test and test output routines.

## General troubleshooting

These steps apply to any make and type of printer, and are the items that you should check if you cannot print.

1.  Check the cable connection between the printer and the computer. Make certain that the parallel cable is connected securely to the printer, and clipped into place. At the computer, the connector should be secured with its bolts. If the fastenings seem sound and nothing else appears to be wrong, try another printer cable in case the existing cable is defective. This is rare, but it does happen.

2.  Make certain that the printer drivers are installed by clicking on the *Printers* item in Windows Control Panel. The printer you are using should be named (right-click on the name) as the default printer for Windows. If your printer is not listed then the printer driver is probably not installed.

3.  If the driver is installed and selected as the default you may find that you can print, but not correctly. You can try using another printer driver, because some drivers that you get on discs may be faulty. Try another driver from the same family of printers, and if this improves the condition, it's likely that the normal driver is at fault. Make sure you are using the most recent version of the printer driver. See Appendix B for Web sites maintained by manufacturers.

## Troubleshooting your PC printer

## Error messages

A printer problem may be accompanied by an error message, and the nature of the message can be a useful clue to what is wrong. The following messages are often seen, and they are followed here by suggestions on tackling the problem.

*The printer is off-line or not selected*:

Printer is off-line, connecting cable is faulty or plugs loose, or your printer has not been selected as the default printer for Windows or there is no driver for the MS-DOS application you are using and printing from.

*Write fault error writing device. Abort, retry, ignore, fail?:*

The LPT1 port has not been set up in the CMOS RAM page, or the cable(s) to the parallel port socket are not correctly connected. Remember that there may be an internal connection to the printer socket from the motherboard of the computer.

*Cannot locate printer on LPT1:*

The printer may be plugged into the wrong port on the back of the computer, it is not the default printer for Windows, the cable is not connected correctly, or the printer is not switched on.

*Printer is out of paper or not connected*:

Check that there is paper in the feeder for the printer and that the paper is not jammed. Check also that the printer power is on and data cable is correctly connected.

## Getting assistance

Diagnostic software can often be very useful if you suspect that something is wrong with the printer port setup, but you need to know what you are looking for. Your Windows or MS-DOS software at one time included a diagnostic called MSD (Microsoft System Diagnostics) and this can be run from a DOS command line by typing in the command *msd*. Later versions of Windows 95 (and Windows 98) did not place MSD on your hard drive because diagnostics were included as part of the operating system itself — see any good book on Windows 95 or Windows 98 for details. Either MSD or the Windows diagnostics will find and report on any problems with the printer port. See below on how to find the msd program on the Windows 95 CD-ROM disc.

For Windows 95, click on Control Panel and then *System*. In the System window click on *Ports* and then on *LPT1*. If LPT1 is not listed then this port is not installed. If LPT1 appears you can click on Properties — Resources to read the address range that is used and to see if there is any conflict reported. Windows 98 uses a similar but more comprehensive scheme.

- Once you have your printer working, use the Control Panel — System pane to print a complete diagnosis for your computer. Prepare your printer with a full stack of paper. Select *Computer* at the top of the list, and then click the *Print* button. Note that this is a large printout and you may have to renew the paper if you have not filled the feeder. Keep this printout for future reference.

More useful information is contained on the Windows 95 CD-ROM (and also on the Windows 98 version). You can find the MSD program on the folder **\other\msd**, and there is a diagnostic program that asks you to describe your problem and guides you through problem solving solutions.

This is in the folder **\other\misc\epts** and the program is called **epts.exe**. If you locate this (with the CD in the drive) using Explorer, you can click on epts.exe. This will issue a report on your default printer setup, and also show a chart of problems so that you can click on the difficulty that you have encountered and get advice.

## Troubleshooting your PC printer

## Odd problems

No matter how methodical you are you can be caught out by odd problems that occur only with some combinations of printer and driver. Here is one example of a problem that often seems intractable.

### Print spooling

When you print, the default setting is to use spooling, meaning that the printer codes are held in the memory of the computer and fed to the printer from there. This allows you to get on with other work, and if spooling is disabled you will not be able to use your computer for anything else while printing is in progress.

Some of the early versions of Windows 95 printer drivers seemed to have a spooling problem concerning the way the data is organised. When you install a printer into Windows 95 or Windows 98 the default for some printers is the **EMF** coding setting. The alternative is the setting marked as **RAW**.

If you encounter problems, notably with some Hewlett-Packard models and using Word-7, try printing directly to the port (not spooling). This can be enabled on the Details — Spool Settings pane of the printer Properties (right click on the printer name in Control Panel — Printers) by setting to *Print directly to printer*. If this solves the problems, but ties up your computer, set the Spool Settings *Spool Data Format* to RAW rather then to EMF, and try this.

### Note: MS-DOS users only

If you suspect that printer problems are caused by software conflict, boot the system clean by using the minimum size of Config.sys and Autoexec.bat files. With MS-DOS running, type the command:

Copy config.sys lpt1

and press the Enter key. This should print the Config.sys file on your printer. For a laser printer you may first need to type:

Mode lpt1:,,p  (press ENTER key)

before you use the Copy command.

If the printer deals with this correctly the problem is likely to be a software conflict caused by a setting in the Autoexec.bat or Config.sys file. You will need to consult a good text on MS-DOS to find which command is likely to be the cause of the conflict.

# 4 Impact dot-matrix printers

## Principles

The modern impact dot-matrix printer, usually simply called dot-matrix, uses a print-head that can control a vertical set of metal pins (typically 9, 24 or even 48) which are fired at an ink-impregnated, or carbon, ribbon that is placed between the paper and the print-head. The pins are arranged in one or more vertical rows and the print-head is moved back and forward across the paper to form images.

In the past, other forms of dot-matrix printer have used systems called *comb matrix* or *shuttle matrix*. The comb matrix printer uses a horizontal row, or *comb*, of pins so that it can print a single row of dots very rapidly. If the row of pins is shorter than the page width the comb moves (or shuttles) to and fro as needed to print all the dots for one line of a page. These systems allow the paper to move almost continuously, so that these methods are used for high speed matrix printers. A similar arrangement is used in LED-bar laser printers.

The advantage of the impact dot-matrix printer as compared to older types (and to such devices as the daisywheel printer) is that the shapes that are produced by firing the pins and moving the head can be controlled entirely by software, allowing the printer to produce different character fonts and graphics shapes.

An important advantage of the impact printer, as compared to modern laser and inkjet types is that the impact printer can be used to print carbon copies together with the original top copy. These printers are often used tractor-fed with continuous paper, but most models can handle single sheets and labels as well. Few, however, are fitted with a single page feeder as a standard item, and adding such a feeder can be remarkably expensive.

# Impact dot-matrix printers

The impact dot-matrix is more closely related to a typewriter than other printers, and the platen roller has a hand-wheel at each side so that the paper can be fed in and moved on manually. This allows you to use a dot-matrix printer in much the same way as a typewriter, and makes it much easier to position paper so that, for example, you do not print over a logo or a heading. This allows you to use a dot-matrix printer with very simple software, including very short programs that use the printer as a typewriter. Laser and inkjet printers use automatic single-sheet feeders, and have no provision for manual movement of paper. Only the more elaborate types of word processor programs will allow for precise positioning of the print.

Because printing makes use of this impact system, dot-matrix printers are noisier than other printers. Some claim to use a quiet mode, but it's quiet only in comparison to a daisywheel (or a machine-gun).

The performance of a dot-matrix printer is usually quoted in terms of characters per second (cps). The rate is usually quoted for a built-in font, and will be different if you use the TrueType fonts of Windows. Sometimes several rates are quoted for different fonts and sizes. This makes it difficult to compare printing speeds with laser and inkjet types which usually quote speed as pages per minute of average content.

## Construction

Dot-matrix printers, like all electronic printers, contain a power supply that supplies the low-voltage supplies for the needles of the print-head and the electronic circuits that control the mechanism. The printer contains a main *logic board* that controls all the actions of the printer, and this translates the codes coming to it from the computer into signals that determine which pins are fired and how far the print-head is moved for the next set of marks. The print-head consists of miniature solenoids (electromagnets) that fire the pins on to the ribbon.

The *carriage* is the holder for the print head, and it moves left and right, usually driven by a belt which is in turn controlled by a miniature electric motor (a servo motor) under the control of the main logic board. The position of the carriage can be signalled to the main logic board either from the position of the belt, or by using some form of sensor. Miniature push-button switches (microswitches) are often used to ensure that the carriage does not attempt to move too far.

In addition to moving the carriage, the ribbon has to be moved past the print-head. This is done by using a shaft that engages into the ribbon cartridge and which is turned as the print-head moves.

The paper also has to be moved, and this is done on most dot-matrix printers by using a roller called the *platen*. The paper is sandwiched between the platen and a smaller sprung roller, and the platen is driven by another electric motor. If tractor feed is used, a pair of toothed wheels, one on either side of the platen, is driven along with the platen. The platen drive motor can operate in small steps in either direction, and some graphics printing calls for the platen rotation to be reversed at intervals.

Sensors that feed signals to the main logic board are used to detect if there is paper in the printer, and if the paper has fed on by one line (line-feed), or by one sheet (form-feed). If tractor feed is used, sensors are also used to detect the end of a page so that the continuous paper can be run on to the start of the next page

## Number of pins

The number of pins in the print-head is an important factor in dot-matrix printer design. The minimum number for good printing is nine, and using nine pins allows the print-head to be constructed more easily and in a robust form. You will find, therefore, that dot-matrix printers that are intended for heavy text use are usually 9-pin types, and this robust construction is reflected in high prices, since these are the printers intended to use in offices, spending all day printing multi-part forms on continuous paper.

Nine-pin printers designed for lighter use are generally rather slower and are not ideal when detailed graphics have to be printed. The ability of such a printer to produce fine detail (high resolution) is determined by the diameter of the dot that each pin produces, and a resolution of 180 dots per inch is about as fine as you get. Obviously, you need suitable software to control the printer at this level, and for some mechanisms this is almost impossible, restricting the resolution to lower figures. When elaborate fonts are used or when detailed graphics have to be printed, the nine-pin printer is slow.

This led to the production of 24-pin heads, using two slightly offset banks of 12-pins each, and with pins of a smaller diameter. Typical pin diameters are less than that of a human hair, making the head assembly rather more delicate than its 9-pin counterpart. These 24-pin printers can produce finer detail in drawings and better-looking fonts, and at the same time operate at a higher speed that the 9-pin counterpart, so that 24-pin machines enjoyed some success for a time, though they were later challenged by inkjet machines.

One drawback about the 24-pin type of design is that the wear on the ribbon is much greater, and the thinner needles tend to cause ribbons to tear, so that they eventually jam. A few 48-pin machines were produced, but by that time the impact dot-matrix printer was being superseded by the inkjet type.

# Troubleshooting your PC printer

## Noise

All dot-matrix printers are noisy. The motors whirr and the switches click, and the hammering of the pins sets up a buzzing sound that is instantly recognisable once you have heard it. The early models could set up a din that made the office sound like a sawmill, but the noise level of later models was considerably lower. At one time, silencing boxes could be bought for daisywheel and dot-matrix printers, but these are no longer needed for the quieter models sold today.

Nevertheless if you do a large amount of printing with a dot-matrix machine you should make sure that the noise is not being exaggerated by a resonant surface. Office suppliers still sell felt pads that were intended to reduce the noise of typewriters, and these can be used to the same purpose for dot-matrix printers. Placing a pad under the printer lessens the reverberation of the desk or table, but you may need to take care if there is any chance of blocking air vents. Check with your printer manual to find if there is any prohibition on placing felt pads under the printer.

## Ribbons

Ribbons are as essential to the dot-matrix printer as toner is for the laser printer and ink for the inkjet. Now that fewer dot-matrix printers are sold, ribbon prices are more reasonable than they once were, and some machines get a very high print mileage on a ribbon. In addition, ribbon prices are lower than they were before they had any competition from low-priced inkjet and laser printers.

In general, a ribbon is contained in a cartridge in an endless loop and is crumpled to fit into the cartridge. Small gearwheels inside the cartridge feed the ribbon across the print-head, and on some printers the ribbon cartridge is skewed slightly to ensure that most of the width of the ribbon is used. Other designs make use of only a small ribbon width.

You should beware of dry ribbons, because the printer uses the ink as a form of lubrication for the print-head as well as providing the marking on the paper. You should keep a supply of spare ribbons, but do not on any account take a ribbon out of its packing until it is needed, otherwise it can dry out. Though you are ritually told to use only genuine replacement ribbons, you will probably find sources of ribbons at much lower prices. You may even find that these compatible ribbons are manufactured by the same suppliers as provide the 'genuine' variety. The well-known names of suppliers of typewriter ribbons are not likely to provide ribbons that are inferior in any way.

You can re-ink ribbons if you find that the cost is excessive, and the methods are detailed in Chapter 5. Another option is to spray the ribbon with a silicone lubricant, such as the well-known WD40, to encourage ink to spread from the unused parts of the ribbon to the more heavily trodden parts.

In general, the longest ribbon life is achieved using full-width ribbons with a 9-pin print-head, and the shortest life is associated with the use of a small cartridge that moves with the head of a 24-pin printer.

## Multi-part paper

One of the main reasons for using a dot-matrix printer is that you can use multi-part stationery, meaning layers of paper with carbon or paper between, or layers of NCR (No Carbon Required) paper. You may not, however, realise how restricted this can be.

The use of multi-part stationery is easiest when the stationery is continuous, sold in a large and costly tractor-fed roll. Tractor feeding is very precise, and because all the sheets of the multi-layer roll are perforated, there is no problem about keeping the sheets together.

## Troubleshooting your PC printer

This is seldom true if you try to work with single sheets. On most printers only the platen roller is powered, so that what very often happens is that the top sheet moves further than the others — sometimes *only* the top sheet moves. This, of course, makes the use of multi-part stationery impractical.

Not all printers are equally bad in this respect, but if you are thinking of using multi-part single pages you should make sure that your printer will cope, and if you are choosing a printer you should see it being operated with the pages you intend to feed through it. Some models apply power to the roller that is held against the platen, and this ensures that the layers stay together.

### Paper path and thickness

All dot-matrix printers rely on wrapping the paper around at least half the diameter of the platen, so that some curling is inevitable. A typical paper path is illustrated here.

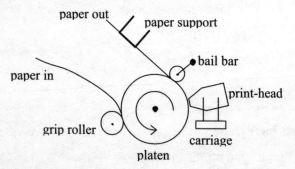

This puts a limit on the thickness of paper that can be used, and in the usual terms of grams per square metre $(g/m^2)$, a figure of around 100 is the usual limit. At the other end of the scale, paper thinner than 60 $g/m^2$ will feed without problems, but may be pierced by the print needles.

Most varieties of dot-matrix printers have a paper-thickness adjustment which also serves as an adjustment for impact strength. You can move the carriage position relative to the paper, and if you keep the carriage close to the paper the impact of the pins is less than if they are allowed a greater distance to accelerate. Nevertheless, the thickness of paper that you can use is determined more by the amount of bending you can tolerate rather than by what adjustments of space between carriage and platen you can make.

## Drivers

The availability of drivers is very important for dot-matrix printers, and some makes suffer from having no driver in the Windows set. The early versions of Windows 95, for example, had no drivers for any of the Star printers, though this was remedied in the later versions of Windows 95, and Windows 98 offers several hundred more driver options.

Fortunately, dot-matrix printers have for a long time been designed to emulate either the Epson 9-pin or the IBM 24-pin ProPrinter types, and this means that no matter how old or obscure your dot-matrix printer is you will always be able to print to the same standard as either of these machine types.

The snag here is that the emulation is not always perfect, and though text printing is always more or less guaranteed, graphics printing may be less certain. All you can do is to create a test page and try printing it with different emulations and different drivers until you get acceptable results.

See Appendix B for manufacturers' Web sites, many of which will provide drivers by downloading.

# 5 Dot-matrix problems

Dot-matrix printers are renowned for having a long trouble-free life, but problems can arise. These are usually related to ribbons, dirt, and drivers rather than to mechanical wear or breakdown. We'll look at some specific advice on maintenance later, but begin by examining some problems and their causes.

These are listed in rough order of decreasing seriousness, starting with a totally dead printer. The causes are listed, but do not assume that knowing the cause will enable you to sort out the problem unless you have experience in repairing mechanisms of this type and also access to spares. For most users, anything involving motors and logic boards will require expert attention.

One point concerning print-head to platen distance is important. If the platen gap is too wide, the pins can extend too far from their guides and break when they are fired. If the gap is too narrow, pins can jam, particularly when printing vertical lines (when a set of adjacent pins are fired). If the gap is adjustable, do not adjust it beyond the limits specified by the manufacturer.

### Printer dead

There is no motor movement, no indicator lights, and no printing. Check first that the power cable is connected and that power is switched on. If power is reaching the printer, then the fault is likely to be a main internal fuse, or a logic board which you cannot deal with yourself.

### Power indicator on, no printing

Check that the printer is on line. Check that the data cable is correctly connected. Try a self-test. If the self-test fails, then the logic board may have failed. If the self-test works and the printer has a data connection and is on line, check for any safety interlocks that prevent printing when a cover is raised or when the carriage is pulled away from the platen for paper loading.

## Impact but carriage does not move

If the pins are hitting the ribbon, but all of the print is in one place because the carriage is not moving, look for anything that might be jamming the carriage. **Be careful** — switch off power before handling the carriage. Check that the drive belt for the carriage is intact, that it is in contact with its driving wheel, and that none of the gears between the driving wheel and the motor are out of mesh or broken. Other possibilities are a burned-out motor or a faulty logic board.

## Pins and carriage move, platen roller does not

Look at the drive (usually gear wheels) for the platen. If these are in mesh, switch off and see if you can move the platen by hand. If the platen is free to move and all the gearing is working suspect a burned-out platen motor or a faulty logic board.

## Printer working but paper does not feed through

The platen may not be gripping the paper (check that the bail bar that holds the paper against the platen is down against the paper), or the paper may be jammed.

## Printer working but ribbon is not feeding:

This will cause the print to become faint after a few words have been printed. The usual cause is a jamming ribbon, so try another ribbon. If this also refuses to feed, suspect the belt and/or gears the drive the ribbon.

## White lines across page

This indicates that a pin is not working. Sometimes this effect is noticeable only as missing tops and bottoms (ascenders and descenders) on letters, but it will be very much easier to see if you print graphics. Try cleaning the print-head. If this has no effect, the print-head may be faulty,

# Troubleshooting your PC printer

or there may be a disconnection in the cable that connects the print-head to the logic board. A more remote possibility is that the logic board is faulty.

## Printer stops before page end

This can happen when your printer is set up for continuous tractor feed, but you are using single sheets. For tractor feed, the printer needs to have an end-of-paper detector activated so that it will stop when the continuous paper runs out. If this detector is not disabled, it will stop the printer working at about 70 millimetres before the end of any single page.

## Squeaks and groans

When a printer is no longer in the first flush of its youth, you are likely to hear a few squeaks and groans, due mainly to the plastic parts being strained. Do not use paper that is too thick, because this will often cause groaning noises as well as straining the printer. If you can locate a noise to a bearing, a light spray of WD40 will often work wonders, but be careful that no spray reaches parts that depend on friction, such as the platen. Cover the platen before spraying anywhere near it.

## Printing with no paper

This can happen on some printers when the end of paper detector has been disabled. Most printers have another paper detector that will not allow printing unless paper is present, but some older models do not use this refinement. Always switch off the printer before you insert paper.

## Remedial and servicing actions

You have to decide for yourself what sort of servicing you are prepared to carry out on your printer. If you have reasonably good DIY skills you can certainly work on items such as head cleaning, ribbon inking, roller cleaning, belt replacement and even possibly head replacement, but you should fight shy of anything that involves working with the

48

logic board or that requires large-scale dismantling of the mechanism. If you are determined to become skilled in printer servicing, make sure that you have all the relevant information from the manufacturer — this is not easy to obtain because it is usually available only to the trade, but you may find sites on the Internet that contain the details.

**Remember that all servicing actions should be carried out with the printer disconnected from the mains and also from the data cable. Do not service a printer that has just been used, because the print-head and some other parts will be hot.**

### Head cleaning

The print-head on an old and much-used printer will eventually become clogged with dried up ink and dust. This jams the pins, which then fire erratically, causing printed output to contain white lines or spots.

Cleaning is a messy but comparatively simple operation that can often clear up problems of print quality on a printer that has previously worked well. If a new printer has problems, return it while it is under guarantee, because it is likely that the problems are not simply due to a dirty print-head.

You will need some cleaning liquid, a small cup such as an egg-cup, kitchen roll, WD40 and a screwdriver. The cleaning liquid is *isopropanol* (isopropyl alcohol), which is used in car windscreen wash fluid and in more pure form sold for cleaning spectacle lenses. The isopropanol sold for car windscreen wash is dyed blue, and this blue dye (used to make the liquid undrinkable) can leave a sticky deposit, so use this liquid only in an emergency.

- Make sure first that the printer is switched off and has its cables disconnected. Don't just disconnect the power cable, because if you move the printer around with the data cable connected there is a risk of straining the data cable and causing some disconnections inside (giving you a new set of faults to worry about).

Start by disconnecting the ribbon cable from the print-head. Note which way round this is connected and look for any retaining clips. Now remove the print-head. Some printers have the print-head bolted to the carriage, others use metal or plastic clips.

Now pour a small amount of cleaning liquid, about 6 millimetres depth, into the egg-cup or whatever container you are using.. Put the print-head nose down into the liquid, but only until the liquid touches the pins. You must not immerse the whole print-head in the liquid. Allow it to soak for a couple of minutes.

Now take the head out of the liquid and press it gently against the kitchen roll. It will leave an ink-stain, and you should repeat these actions until the head leaves little or no stain on the roll. You can then replace the head on the carriage and re-connect the ribbon cable. Do not replace the ribbon.

Now put the printer into normal position, load normal typing paper into it, apply the power cable (not the data cable) and carry out a self-test with no ribbon. This should get rid of any residual ink in the pins

Load paper and execute a self test without a ribbon present. Look at the results. If there has been a large amount of dried ink in the head you might have to repeat the cleaning action. An old toothbrush can be useful for a head that cannot be cleaned by soaking.

Once the pins are ink free, spray the end of the head lightly with the WD40. Some makers provide a lubrication point on the head, and if this is present, oil using only the lubricant (usually a silicone oil) that the manufacturer recommends. If you have no manufacturer's data, try the type of oil that is sold for lubricating electric shavers.

## Head replacement

If you can remove a head for cleaning you can replace a head, but you have to be absolutely certain that the old head is, in fact, faulty. Each pin of a print-head is controlled by a separate power transistor on the main logic board. A faulty transistor can prevent a pin from firing, and installing a new head will not correct the fault, and the transistor fault can even damage the new head. Unless you have a tester that can check out the signals to the pins and indicate any transistor faults, do not replace a head for yourself.

## Drive belts

Drive belts fitted to modern printers are usually toothed belts which do not slip and provide very precise positioning. They are usually automatically tensioned and need no adjustment, so that the only servicing actions are the replacement of a broken belt or to replace a belt that has come adrift from a toothed wheel (perhaps because of a paper jam or because you forgot to remove a staple or a paperclip from the paper).

Do not rush into replacing a broken belt. You need first to get the correct replacement item, and you also need to find out just how much has to be dismantled in order to replace the belt. If in doubt, send the printer to an approved repairer. Replacing a carriage drive belt can be particularly difficult, and some printers are much more awkward for this type of replacement than others.

## Ribbon drives

Ribbon drive is normally done using a toothed shaft that engages in the ribbon cartridge, and the gears that drive this shaft may be accessible. It is unusual to have any problem with these gears, and if there is no drive to the ribbon cartridge you should check first that the shaft is engaging

# Troubleshooting your PC printer

correctly in the ribbon cartridge and that all the other driven parts are working.

Check if you can see the gears that nothing is jammed in them — loose items such as paperclips seem to be irresistibly attracted to nylon gears. If a gearwheel is damaged or broken it will have to be replaced, and this is usually a job for the expert unless you are skilled in repairing small mechanisms and have access to both spares and information.

## Jamming ribbon

A jamming ribbon is uncommon on the older type of ribbon cartridge (typically on the old Epson RX and MX models) that extends the whole width of the platen. By contrast, the small ribbon cartridges that are fitted to 24-pin printers and which move with the carriage as much more likely to jam.

The ribbon is a continuous loop, and if the seams start to come adrift it is almost certain to jam. The ribbon is not neatly folded inside the cartridge, and in the smaller cartridges particularly it can become pinched and so jam. The usual cause is that the ribbon, which is normally held between a couple of plastic wheels, starts to fold so that a folded piece catches between the wheels.

Unless you enjoy getting your hands dirty, the easiest way out is simply to replace the ribbon cartridge. For the smaller cartridges, recovery from a jam can be difficult, and the ribbon will almost certainly jam again soon. If you have no spare, you may want to unjam the ribbon, and if your printer uses the longer cartridge type that does not move then it may be worth while to unjam it.

Remove the ribbon cartridge while the printer is switched off. Place the cartridge on a spread out newspaper. Examine the cartridge — you will find that the bottom part is a single moulding, but there is a separate lid that clips on. This can be removed using a knife blade, easing up each clip until the top falls off. Unless you have some experience, it is likely that some ribbon will spill out also, and that's where the newspaper comes in useful.

Once you can see the drive wheels for the ribbon, you should be able to find the jam. Use tweezers to ease the jammed ribbon out of the wheels, and to replace any of the ribbon that has spilled out of the cartridge. You do not need to have the ribbon neatly folded, but you need to be sure that it is not so badly positioned that it will jam again. Now replace the top of the cartridge and make sure that all the clips are in place. If a clip is damaged, use Sellotape to hold the top of the cartridge firmly down.

Replace the cartridge in the printer, and with luck you should be able to finish the printing you had started. In many cases, the ribbon will last until it needs replacement in the normal way.

## Roller staining

If you find that printed paper is emerging from the printer with stains, the first thing to look for is ink on the platen or any other rollers (on the bail bar, for example) that are in contact with the paper. The usual cause of ink on the platen is accidental printing with no paper, and if the staining is bad and cannot be removed simply by running some sheets of paper through the printer, you must remove the platen and clean it.

The platen roller usually clips out easily, though you might need to remove retaining springs, and cleaning it is also straightforward. Use a cloth moistened with isopropanol (see head cleaning), and rub until no more ink appears on the cloth. Dry with a kitchen roll, and make sure that no dust, cloth or paper fragments are sticking to the platen roller. Replace it, and do some printing to see if the fault is now cured.

## Troubleshooting your PC printer

### Driver or emulation problems

The usual sign of a driver or emulation problem is that gibberish is printed. This may apply to all of your text, or just to some portions such as graphics, text in italics or bold, or underlined text. The obvious solution is to try another driver or emulation, and it is unusual to be unable to find nothing that works.

Most of the problems that have been common in the past have been encountered when printing from MS-DOS applications, and many of these, such as printing text characters instead of graphics shapes, simply do not occur when you print from Windows. The use of Windows has also removed the old problem of printing another character (such as $ or #) instead of the £ sign. If you are using an MS-DOS application, make sure that you have a suitable driver, and you may also have to set switches on your printer to ensure that it is using the correct character set (with a £ sign). None of this is normally needed if you print from Windows.

One exception that sometimes arises when you print from a document obtained from someone else is that the last character in each word is a foreign character. This happens when the document has been typed using WordStar, and is fairly uncommon now. The remedy is to convert the WordStar codes to the ones used in your own word processor, either using a WordStar filter to read the document, or using a separate *WordStar to Text* utility program that you can find in shareware lists.

### Re-inking ribbons

Re-inking ribbons is a practice that is not exactly smiled upon by manufacturers for obvious reasons, and you will often hear comments about risking the life of your printer. All I can say is that my 14 year old Epson has survived, and the Star of 1986 vintage looks like surviving for the same length of time. At the current prices of compatible ribbons you need to be rather parsimonious to need to re-ink ribbons, but there is no reason why you should not know how to go about it.

Re-inking starts with opening the ribbon cartridge as described earlier under the heading of *jamming ribbon*. Once the cartridge is open you can spray either ink or WD40, and for ribbons that were installed new, the WD40 spray is often all that is needed to get another lifetime from the ribbon. The solvent in the spray dissolves ink from the unused part of the ribbon, and this solution then soaks into the used part, providing new ink.

For subsequent treatments, you can continue to use WD40 for a considerable time on the larger cartridges that are used on the older Epson printers, but at some stage there is simply not enough ink left anywhere on the ribbon, and only a fresh supply of ink will do. In the past I have used ink supplied for ink-stamp pads, poured sparingly on the ribbon, but in the 1980s several firms supplied ink spray for ribbons, and this may still be available, but I have not seen it advertised.

Another possibility, if you use ribbons intensively, is a ribbon inking machine, and this is still advertised by:

Beach Imaging Ltd.,
243 Eltham High St.,
London SE9 1TX
Tel: 0181 850 8344
E-mail beachimaging@enterprise.net

who may also be able to provide suitable ink. Searches on the Web do not reveal other UK sources, though it is possible that overseas sources might exist.

# 6 Inkjet printers

Inkjet printers have largely superseded impact dot-matrix types for printing with single sheets of paper (**not** multi-part stationery), and particularly for graphics and colour printing. The advantages are fast and quiet (though see later) printing, with low machine costs. The disadvantages are that consumable costs are high even for text, and can be *very* high if you want to print copies of photographs.

There are two main forms of inkjet printers, the bubblejet type developed by Canon and Hewlett-Packard (the name 'bubblejet' is a trademark of Canon), and the piezoelectric type developed by Epson and used in their *Stylus* range. The printing mechanisms (or *engines*) made by Canon and H-P are sold to other manufacturers, so that any inkjet printer under any other name is likely to use one of these engines. Epson engines are not used by any other manufacturers.

## Bubblejet and piezo types

The bubblejet printer relies on a principle that is said to have been discovered accidentally when a soldering iron was placed on a hypodermic syringe. The heating of the liquid in a narrow-bore tube has the effect of vaporising some of the liquid, so that the pressure of the vapour shoots out a small drop of liquid, and this is replaced by more liquid when the tube cools again. The remarkable feat has been to mass-produce these heated nozzles in a very small size and in a matrix form of jets in a vertical line, using 12, 24 or 48 nozzles in a print-head.

The piezoelectric print-head works in quite a different way. A few crystals of materials, either natural like quartz, or artificial like barium titanate, alter their size slightly when an electrical voltage is applied across them. Drilling a hole through a crystal and feeding ink through this hole will allow the ink to be squeezed out when an electrical voltage is applied across the crystal, and this technology also can be miniaturised to provide print-heads.

- Neither of these systems could have been used to any great extent if the ink technology had not moved as fast as the technology of the mechanism. The ink must be fluid enough to pass easily through the very fine tubes in the head, yet it must dry almost instantly when it reaches the paper so that it does not smudge. Inks contain very small particles, and if the particle size is not kept small, clogging of jets is likely.

The bubble-jet is the older of the methods, and it has been refined to a remarkable extent. The printing action is quiet (though the motors that drive the carriage and the platen roller are not) and the printed output is excellent, comparable with a good laser printer. Early types were limited to 300 × 300 dots per inch, but later types have stretched this to 600 or more dots per inch in each direction.

The main snag is that the nozzles tend to become blocked, so that a new print-head has to be bought at intervals. Some types, notably the H-P DeskJet models, manufacture the nozzles and ink cartridge in one piece, so that you are renewing the nozzles each time you put in a new ink cartridge. Others, like Canon, manufacture separate units so that you can renew the ink cartridge several times before the nozzle block has to be renewed. Refilling cartridges is frowned on by the manufacturers, but is almost universally practised because it reduces the otherwise high running costs.

The piezoelectric type of system normally has a fixed nozzle head assembly with replaceable cartridges of ink. The nozzle assembly is said to have a long life, but ink cartridges are very expensive, and this is an incentive to refill. My own experience has been that the text print quality is not as high as that of bubblejet printers on ordinary paper, and this is

## Troubleshooting your PC printer

particularly noticeable under slight magnification. Graphics quality in colour, using coated paper, is excellent.

## Mechanism

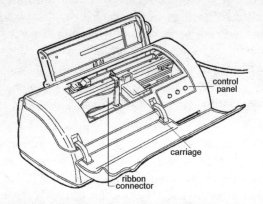

The mechanism of the inkjet printer owes a lot to that of the impact dot-matrix type, but with the important difference that because there is no impact there is no need to have a solid platen supporting the paper. This permits the use of a light flat plastic sheet supporting the paper, and results in a much straighter and simpler paper path.

The print-head and ink cartridge (whether combined or separate) are clipped to a carriage (see illustration) that is moved from side to side by a toothed belt, and the electrical signals are sent to the head by a ribbon cable. The carriage contains the electrical contact for the head, so that the ribbon cable does not need to be detached when a print-head is replaced.

A control panel provides buttons and warning lights, and provides for such actions as cartridge replacement, on/off line, paper form feed, and reset. The on/off switch can be on this panel or separate; it is sometimes omitted altogether and the printer goes into stand-by mode when no commands have been sent to it for some time.

## Mono and colour

The dot-matrix type of printer could at one time be obtained in colour form, using a three-colour ribbon, but the availability of colour inkjet machines put an end to this, because the quality of colour printing from impact dot-matrix machines was rather poor.

Colour inkjet machines originally used a combination print-head and cartridge assembly with three coloured inks and three lines of nozzles. The ink colours are yellow, cyan and magenta, and all three mixed ought to produce black, but in practice produce only a dark brown. Because of this and the fact that printers generally need black more than they need colour, modern colour inkjets use separate black and colour head assemblies.

Colour inkjets can provide passable colour illustrations to newspaper standards on plain paper, and rather better results of special coated paper, which can be frighteningly expensive, approaching £1 per sheet. What they cannot do, despite claims, is to provide results that match a good colour photograph, and this is because of the limitations of colour mixing.

Given three basic colours, the obvious process would be to produce any other colour by mixing the inks, but the ink dries so quickly that it cannot mix on the paper and is not mixed in the jet nozzles. Colours other than the yellow, cyan and magenta ones are therefore produced by dithering, meaning that dots of the primary colours are placed close to each other to give the effect to the eye of a different colour. This form of colour mixing is not new; it is the principle used for colour TV in which each dot on the screen is either blue, green or red.

- Note that the primary colours for light projection are blue, green and red, but for reflecting light from paper we use yellow, cyan and magenta.

# Troubleshooting your PC printer

The colour resolution for a printer is therefore lower than its resolution for monochrome, a fact that is also true of TV. TV gets round this by using black and white for edges of shapes, so that these are precise, and colour for fills, which need not be so precise. This relies on the fact that the resolution of the human eye for colours, particularly red, is much lower than it is for black and white

A heavily dithered colour image can look quite acceptable if you do not examine it in detail, so that highly magnified images have to be avoided. The approach used for more realistic colour is to use very high resolution, such as 1400 dots per inch, so that the dithered image is still reasonably sharp. This, however, is not possible at present on ordinary paper, hence the coated variety that is essential for *photo-real* printing. Coating is essential to get brightness of colour because there is more reflected light from the coating.

Some modern inkjets are now using up to six colour heads to produce better results from dithering, but this obviously leads to higher running costs.

- The only type of printer that can truly mix colours without dithering is the dye-sublimation type, in which the inks are vaporised and mixed in vapour form.

Undoubtedly one effect of the intensive advertising of colour inkjet printers is to raise expectations much too high, so that users tend to be disappointed at the results they obtain. This is not surprising, because colour printing of any kind is an art rather than an exact science, and cannot be reduced to a set of rules.

## Noise levels

The sound level of a typical bubble-jet type of printer is uncannily low, and only the whine of the electric motors reveals that the printer is working at all. The piezoelectric type is much noisier, and some examples are as loud as a dot-matrix printer at full blast, with the penetrating buzz of the piezoelectric devices being easily heard over the sound of the electric motors.

## Paper path

The paper path of inkjet printers is often much more straight than that of dot-matrix or laser types, and on some models quite thick card (up to 500 g/m$^2$) can be printed. The paper path varies considerably from one model to another, however, and if you want to be able to use thick material you need to look for the manufacturer's figures on the permitted thickness. On some models, provision is made for altering the distance between the heads and the paper so that thicker material can be used.

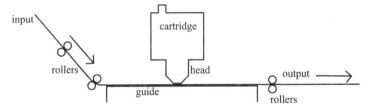

For many machines, the paper path is very similar to that of an impact dot-matrix printer, so that the side of paper that will be printed is the side that faces away from you when you load the feeder. Typically, the paper is bent through an angle of less than 90°, but for thick material it needs to be fed straight, and this increases the *footprint* of the printer on a desk.

## Ink supply

Whatever type of inkjet printer you use, it needs to have some method of holding a supply of ink, and some way of passing the ink from this container, or reservoir, to the print-head. The print-head is then responsible for spitting out drops of ink to the correct points on the paper.

# Troubleshooting your PC printer

With ink contained in a cartridge, there has to be some way of allowing air to enter the cartridge as the ink flows out, otherwise the flow will soon dry up. On the other hand, if the flow of ink is too free, the ink will no longer be totally under control, and it will drip from the jets even when no printing is being done.

The most common method that is used in all types of inkjet machines is to fill the cartridge with a sponge that is then saturated with the ink. This sponge provides enough resistance to the movement of ink to prevent dripping, but the pumping action of the print-head will be enough to overcome this resistance and provide a feed of ink when needed. An air vent allows the air to replace ink as the ink flows out. A few cartridges use a double chamber system, with a reservoir of ink that has to pass through a sponge in the second chamber to reach the print-head.

There is one alternative system used by Hewlett-Packard on some older models, such as the original DeskJet, DesignJet and DeskWriter models using the cartridge type 51626A. This cartridge has no sponge, and the feed of ink is regulated by an ingenious system that uses airbags. The 51626A cartridge contains twice the ink as the discontinued 51608A which it replaced.

The cartridge is maintained internally at a slight negative pressure and as the ink flows, two air bags expand to occupy more space. The expansion of the airbags is controlled by a spring, and a further check on pressure difference is applied by a small diameter hole at the bottom of the cartridge.

This type of cartridge is extensively used on machines that use the H-P engine under other names, see Appendix A. One snag is that the cartridge is, as you would expect, sensitive to changes in air pressure and is likely to leak when there is a rapid change of pressure (don't take your printer on a flight unless you can seal the cartridge). If you try to refill a cartridge of this type you have to be very careful about resealing it after injecting the ink.

## Consumables

The consumables of an inkjet printer are ink cartridges and paper. Supplies for Canon and H-P printers are easy to find, even at local suppliers, but Epson cartridges are not always so easily available. All three cartridge types can be bought as original manufacturer's types or as compatibles, with the compatibles (often from very well-respected sources) considerably cheaper. The prices for Canon cartridges are always lower than for H-P because the Canon type are quoted as ink cartridges only, but the H-P type consist of ink cartridge and heads in one unit. Epson cartridges consist of ink only, but are more expensive that either of the other two, though the compatibles are more affordable.

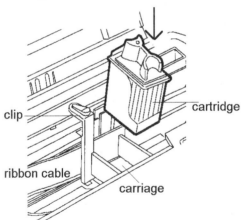

Cartridge replacement, for either main type, is simple. The usual system is to clip the complete cartridge (heads and ink reservoir) into the carriage. Where the ink reservoir is a separate unit, it can usually be replaced without the need to unclip the head unit from the carriage. The illustration shows the Olivetti JP170S system.

# Troubleshooting your PC printer

Plain paper for text printing on all main inkjet types can be ordinary copy-grade paper — you should avoid the very thin *bank* paper because the ink tends to soak into it and be visible on the other side. If your main concern is printing of text, plain or illustrated with line drawings, the use of copy paper at about £3.00 per ream (500 sheets) is perfectly adequate, and no improvement will be noticeable if you use more expensive paper. On the contrary, using thicker paper may cause printer jamming and will reduce the number of sheets that you can put into the feeder, and using coated paper will drive up your printing costs enormously.

- Note that all copy paper of good quality will have one preferred side, and this is the side that should be printed on. The wrapping around a ream of paper will usually carry an arrow that indicates the preferred side, and you should keep the paper in its wrapping so that you do not have to try to remember which side to use.

## High-quality graphics

Where high-resolution graphics or colour printing that uses dithering is required , ordinary copy paper is inadequate and high-quality coated inkjet paper is needed. A typical price at the time of writing is 200 sheets of A4 for £25, but the price of photographic quality paper can go as high as £25 for 15 sheets of A4 — about the same price as photographic paper itself. These prices are obviously geared to one-off prints, but you may need to make several attempts to get the colour rendering you want, so that high-resolution colour printing can be a very costly business. Certainly digital photography has some way to go before it can match the costs and quality of traditional photographic processes.

## Resolution figures

The early inkjet printers produced resolution figures of $360 \times 360$ dots per inch, and at a time when laser printers could boast only $300 \times 300$ resolution, this was a decided step forwards. Inkjets then progressed to $600 \times 600$ resolution, and laser printers followed some time later. Many inkjet printers now feature 720 or 750 dots per inch in each direction, and 1440 dots per inch is now possible on coated paper.

The use of coated paper is the snag, and nothing like 1440 dots per inch can be achieved on ordinary paper even of comparatively good quality. If you assume that the highest resolution you will use for normal purposes is around 600 dots per inch you can save yourself a considerable amount on printer and paper costs.

Some manufacturers quote very high resolutions with the use of *interpolation*. This means altering an image so as to fill in jagged lines and generally smooth the image to look as if it had been produced by a printer with much higher resolution. Never be tempted by these figures, and if you can look at an example of an image printed on plain paper with a typesetter such as the Linotronic with a genuine resolution of 2,400 dots per inch and compare this with the interpolated 2,400 output from an inkjet you will see the difference.

## Speed

The speed of inkjet printers can vary enormously, and the faster the printer the higher the cost. For example, a printer capable of 3–4 pages per minute will sell for around £150–£250, but if you want a speed of 7 pages per minute this will almost double the price.

Speeds are always very controversial, because any quoted speed may be achieved under rather artificial conditions. You will get somewhere close to quoted speeds if you print pages that contain no graphics, and you start timing the page delivery after the first page of a set has been printed. The quoted speeds, however, are useful for comparing printers even if they do not relate well to the speed of printing your typical pages.

# 7 Inkjet problems

Inkjet printers in general feel more fragile and are noticeably lighter than the older models of dot-matrix printers, though some modern low-cost laser printers come close to them in size and weight. This appearance of fragility, often enhanced when you try to open the lid and find that the whole casing flexes noticeably, is deceptive, and an inkjet printer is just as capable of a long working life as the older type of printer.

What is undoubtedly true is that inkjet printers need more care and regular servicing actions, and they cannot be left to run day in, day out, in the way that you will have been accustomed to if you have used a dot-matrix or laser printer. The main troublesome area concerns the print-head and ink-flow, because the rest of the mechanism is the same tried and tested carriage and paper-feed system as used by all dot-matrix types.

Because head problems are so common, some driver software contains diagnostic routines and jet-clearing routines that should be used at intervals. This type of software is particularly important if the print-heads are intended to be used for the life of the printer, as for the Epson Stylus models, but is less important if a new print-head is included as part of a new ink cartridge. You can, however, find that you get jet problems even in the life of one ink cartridge.

What follows, then, is a list, in no particular order, of faults and their causes that you will almost inevitably find at some time occurring on your inkjet printer.

## White streaking

White streaking is a sign of a blocked, dirty, or damaged nozzle, perhaps more than one, and it may be intermittent. The faulty nozzle may be at the top or bottom of the matrix, so that it does not show on text, but appears when you print graphics with solid fills.

- The fault, however, may not be in the nozzle, but in the electrical contacts to the head. Simply removing the whole head and gently wiping these contact can often work wonders, and the manual for your printer should describe the process.

If the fault is not electrical, and you have nozzle clearing software, run it, making certain that you have loaded the printer with scrap paper. Do **not** attempt to run this type of software if you are almost out of ink because it will put more ink than normal through the nozzles, and if you run out of ink in the course of the routine you will end up with several nozzles filled with air, storing up more problems for yourself and probably not clearing the blocked nozzle.

If this has no effect and the print-head is an integral part of the cartridge, then the simplest cure is to install another cartridge and head assembly. For printers in which only the ink cartridge is changed, you should check to find how many times this has been done. Manufacturers often suggest that the head should be changed after three ink cartridges have been used. This probably corresponds to about 3 reams — 1500 sheets — of paper.

If you feel that the head has not reached its ultimate mileage but does not respond to cleaning software, you can try cleaning it for yourself. First of all, try gently pressing an absorbent piece of paper against the head. Beware of kitchen paper and any other paper that has long loose fibres, because these can cause clogging rather than solving it. You can use a synthetic cloth material if you prefer it.

The ultimate treatment, which can be successful when all else has failed is simply to boil your head. This, remember, makes any form of guarantee on the head void, and must **never** be attempted with an Epson piezoelectric head. Use just enough water to cover the head, and keep it simmering in a small saucepan. Keep the head in the water for about five minutes. If this does not show signs of clearing the blockage (check using a good magnifying glass), try boiling the head longer using a strong ammonia solution (add clear ammonia liquid to the simmering water). Do not under any circumstances use the type of household ammonia that is cloudy because it contains soap. Do not try to put the head into use again until it has dried externally.

## Black streaking

Black streaking is a much more unusual fault, and it is always intermittent, sometimes on a few characters, a few words or a few lines per page. If this occurs on a new printer, return the printer under guarantee, because sorting out the problem is by no means easy.

If you are plagued by black streaking on a printer that is out of guarantee, try cleaning the head with a moistened synthetic cloth, taking care not to rub the head, only pat it with the cloth. Rubbing the head can tear off filaments of the material and cause clogging. This treatment can sometimes work if the black streaking is being caused by ink-soaked fibres of paper clinging to the head and being dragged across the page. You might, for example, be using a paper that is too fibrous, or using the wrong side of a paper that is otherwise satisfactory.

- Where your document contains both graphics and text you may see white streaks on the graphics that appear as black streaks on the text beside the graphics. This is not due to paper or blocked nozzles, and is a fault that can only be sorted out by sending the machine to the manufacturers or appointed repairers.

Another possible cause is a fault in the logic board that keeps a nozzle squirting when it should not be. This is definitely a problem that will be costly to deal with because it almost certainly will need the replacement of the logic board, and unless you are an electronics engineer you should not attempt this for yourself even if you can obtain a spare. Always seek the advice of the manufacturers on this type of problem.

## Faint or irregular print

Faint, or a mixture of faint and normal, printing is another common problem, and before you suspect a printer fault you should check that you have not specified draft mode in your driver software. Some bubble-jet types, notably the Olivetti JP170S, provide a draft mode that is only slightly less dark than normal printing, and is quite acceptable for most purposes. By contrast, Epson Stylus models have a draft mode that looks grey and faint and is useful only for unimportant work.

If you see some pieces of faint print and others of normal inking, you should suspect air bubbles in the ink supply. Some printers have software that will pump the ink through the nozzles until the bubbles disappear, others have a manual system that squeezes a plastic delivery pipe (the ink aspirator) until ink appears on the whole length of the tube. This problem is one that is most likely to appear when you have refilled a cartridge for yourself and have not followed the instructions precisely. On some types of refilled cartridge, you are advised to let the cartridge sit for a period of up to several days before you use it.

## Paper handling

The paper handling of inkjet printers is usually excellent, and paper jamming is unusual. The paper path is normally good, with very little bending. If the printer uses a paper output tray, make sure that this is extended far enough for the length of paper that you are using, otherwise the paper will buckle as it comes out and this can cause crumpling and ink streaking.

## Troubleshooting your PC printer

Always observe the instructions relating to paper loading. You are usually advised not to attempt to add sheets to paper that is already in the delivery tray — the correct method is to take all the paper out, add more (the correct way round) and then replace the bundle of paper in the tray. A bundle of paper should be fanned out and then bundled again before loading into the tray, so that there is no tendency for the sheets to stick together.

Envelopes can present another type of problem, and printer manuals can be confusing. You can sometimes see instructions about turning the print heads around (using a lever control) for printing envelopes, but if you print from Word or any other fully-featured word processor you do **not** need to make any form of change to your printer in order to print envelopes. You simply run the envelope-printing routine of your word processor and load in the envelope the way that is illustrated (in Word's Tools — Envelopes and Labels menu, for example).

If you are in doubt, try some practice runs with pieces of paper cut to the size of the envelopes you want to use. The popular DL size of envelope usually has to be fed sideways with the flap away from you, but sometimes the driver suggestions are not correct for your printer, so that practice is useful. You can use either self-sealing or the usual lick and stick type of envelopes on an inkjet printer.

## Cartridge refilling – general

The cost of using an inkjet printer can be considerably reduced if you refill your cartridges, and a substantial industry has grown up around this. As always, manufacturers frown on the practice, and in the UK you will find manufacturers issuing thinly veiled threats that the warranty will be void if you refill your cartridges, or claiming that cartridges cannot possibly be refilled.

In the US, where consumer law is a lot tighter, manufacturers are simply not allowed to make such comments, and they risk being sued by the suppliers of refill kits if they try to restrict warranties. Hewlett-Packard in the USA, for example, state that 'the use of a refilled print cartridge does not affect the warranty unless failure or damage is attributable to it'. Other manufacturers in the USA also follow this line, which reflects the fact that the ink is contained in the cartridge and does not touch any part of the printer itself. A manufacturer, in other words, can quibble about replacing a print-head if unapproved ink has been used, but cannot refuse to implement the warranty on the other parts of the printer.

Another suggestion is that the refill ink is inferior and may cause the jets to clog. This also is a feeble argument, because the ink is as often as not manufactured by the same specialist as supplies the manufacturer, sometimes even to a higher specification.

You may feel that you are prepared to refill a black ink cartridge, but not a colour cartridge on the grounds that the ink colours will be different. In fact, consistency of colour is always a problem, and you can find that two samples of 'genuine' colour cartridges do not match perfectly. These differences can be corrected by using the image software from which you are printing, and refilling a colour cartridge is no more difficult (though it is three times as much effort) as filling a black cartridge.

- The usual cartridge filling method use a hypodermic syringe and needle, and if you are uneasy about possessing such implements in the house you may decide simply to pay the price for compatible cartridges that come ready-filled. You should avoid systems that make use of a squeeze bottle, because ink delivery is not as precise, and the results can be very messy.

## Troubleshooting your PC printer

You should always handle cartridges carefully and avoid touching the metallic parts such as the electrical contacts and (for some types) the nozzles. You can store your refilled cartridges at room temperature in a sealed plastic bag, preferably in a cool place. Try not to keep unfilled cartridges for any length of time, because there is a risk of drying out.

## Outline method

Though there are variations from one type of cartridge to another, the general method is much the same for all, and in particular for all the cartridges that use a sponge to soak up the ink. You have to start with the ink cartridge (which for some models will include the heads) removed from the printer. Consult the manual for your printer for the method, because methods of retaining cartridges vary from one make to another. You should always aim to refill a cartridge before it runs out of ink, and many printers will report the need for ink in reasonable time. This prevents the print head from drying up, which will often result in the heating elements burning out, and it also extends the life of the sponge in the type of cartridge that uses a sponge filling.

Because spilled ink is not easy to remove from furniture or carpets, you should work on an easily cleaned surface. If you work on a table or desk, use a large dinner plate covered with a piece of kitchen paper towel to place the cartridge and inking equipment.

The usual type of sponge-filled cartridge should be filled slowly, and filling stopped or suspended when the cartridge is nearly full. Instructions for specific cartridges will often tell you what amount of ink (such as 20 ml) to use, but this might be too much if the sponge still retains a significant amount of ink. Filling must stop when the sponge is saturated, and you should never have ink slopping about inside the cartridge.

Once you have filled a cartridge you may want to store it so that you always have a reserve in stock. This is simple enough for the type of cartridge that is simply an ink reservoir, but if your cartridges are combined with the print-head you need to be more careful about storing them. You should wipe the print nozzles with a synthetic cloth that has been moistened with cartridge cleaning fluid (obtainable from your ink supplier), tape over the head, and store in a sealed plastic bag in a cool place. Before you use a cartridge/print-head assembly, wipe the head again so as to remove any ink that may have dried on the nozzles.

## Details, general method

Some cartridges have a filling hole that is covered by a sticky label, and you need to pull this label back so that you can see the hole. On some cartridges, you are advised to pierce the plastic cover with the hypodermic needle. The illustration is based on an Epson cartridge.

You need to assemble the syringe and the needle and then fill with the specified quantity of ink. The amount of coloured ink will usually be less than the amount of black ink.

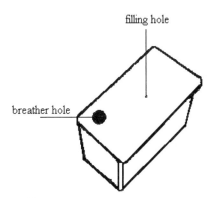

filling hole

breather hole

Now insert the needle through the filling hole or into the specified point on the plastic cover. Your instructions for the cartridge will tell you how far in the needle should be inserted. On some cartridges, you will damage a filter gauze if the needle is inserted more than a few millimetres, on others you can insert the needle beyond the centre of the sponge. You will feel some resistance to the movement of the needle because of the sponge. The further you can insert the needle the better, because this helps to avoid trapped air which will cause air-locks later.

You can now inject the ink, typically 5 ml of coloured ink or 10 ml of black. Stop at once if ink appears at the filling hole. Any unused ink can be returned to the bottle. You must then clean the syringe and needle thoroughly, finishing off with soft or demineralised water (sold for topping up car batteries). You need not use a special flushing solution if you are going to carry out another filling action with a different colour of ink, but its always an advantage to flush the syringe if you are going to store it for the next refill.

• For some cartridges, notably Epson Color 400/600/800 models you are advised to seal the cartridge and store for some time, which can be as long as a week. See the specific instructions for your cartridge.

For most types, once a cartridge has been filled you should replace it on the head or carriage and then run whatever type of priming cycle you would normally use for a replacement cartridge. The priming instructions will be contained in your printer manual, and they may involve using software or pressing a combination of buttons on the printer itself.

## Other types

The refilling procedure for sponge-filled cartridges is very similar for all cartridges of this general kind, but, as noted in Chapter 6, the H-P type 51626A cartridge that is used on a large number of printers (carrying names other than H-P) uses a quite different system for regulating the ink flow. This means that the refilling method, though using the syringe and needle system, is rather different.

You should follow the method that is recommended by your supplier of ink and refilling kit, but the general method is roughly this. You start by removing the cartridge, and taping over the air vent at the bottom and the top centre hole. You can use electrician's insulating tape because this gives a much better seal than masking tape or ordinary Sellotape. You can also use Sellotape mounting pads (cut into small pieces). It is particularly important to get a good seal on the top centre hole.

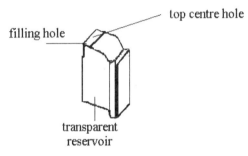

With the cartridge upright, you should now use a ball-point pen or a cocktail stick to push the ball valve at the corner of the top of the cartridge into its holder. You can now refill through this hole, using 40 ml of black ink for the black cartridge. Fill only to the top of the clear plastic area. You now have to insert a plastic plug (supplied in the inking kit) into the hole to seal it. The plug is usually a plastic ball and it should be pushed in until it is flush with the top of the cartridge.

Remove the sealing tapes and stand the cartridge on a paper towel for a few hours until any leakage has subsided. Leakage is the main refilling problem, and you should carefully follow any advice from your ink-kit supplier on this subject if you encounter leakage problems. This may require you to inject air into the top centre hole.

## Troubleshooting your PC printer

### Olivetti JP170S

This printer is remarkable in being the only one that is advertised as being suitable for refilling, though the manual contains the ritual warnings against the practice. Though some charts suggest that this printer uses the 51626A cartridge you will find that the cartridge is sponge filled, and has a filling hole (black) or three filling holes for the colour version. The cartridge takes 12 ml of black ink or 5 ml of each colour. You are advised to refill empty cartridges immediately and not to let them dry out.

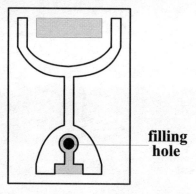

**filling hole**

### Filling problems

The problem that you are most likely to find after refilling a cartridge is that the ink flow is poor, usually due to an air-lock. One point that has already been mentioned is to inject the fresh ink as far into the sponge as possible, but this is not always easy, and you may find that you cannot inject ink, using reasonable pressure, when the needle is deep inside the sponge.

If you have an air-locked cartridge, one effective way of overcoming it is to use the 'tomato ketchup' technique. This has to be done outdoors or in a place where some spattered ink might not the noticed. Hold the cartridge upright, with the delivery pad of ink nozzles (depending on type) downwards. Move your arm downwards, fast, and stop suddenly, so that the ink in the cartridge is forced downwards. Some may leak out, proving that the action was effective and that you have broken the air-lock.

## Other problems

Printers of different manufacture (or badging) use different methods of indicating faults, but the most common is that lights start flashing when a fault occurs. You should keep beside the printer a note of what combinations of flashing light indicate which faults. Some printers use the software to indicate problems; these will be the printers that require a bi-directional printing cable. A few models use a combination of flashing lights and the position of the print-head when the lights start flashing to signal what is wrong. Check with your manual to find out how errors are signalled for your particular model.

### No printing

If the carriage and paper move normally but there is no printing after a cartridge replacement, this is usually because you have not removed the sealing tape from the bottom of the cartridge. If the fault occurs on a cartridge that has been in use for some time the cartridge may be empty, though this will usually have been signalled by indicator lights or software messages before the ink runs out completely. Another possibility is a badly clogged head — try the head cleaning routine.

### Printing garbage

Check that your inkjet is selected in Windows as the default printer. Try printing without using Print Manager of Windows. If this eliminates the problem then use Print Manager only if you are certain that there is ample spare space on the hard drive and that you have a valid TEMP folder for temporary files. This should be registered in the Autoexec.bat file in a line such as:

# Troubleshooting your PC printer

Set temp=C:\temp

and the folder should appear in an Explorer view.

# 8 Laser printers

## Principles

The ultimate in monochrome print quality at the present time can be provided by the laser type of printer, which also includes variants such as LED bar printers and LCD-mask printers. All of these are fast and silent in action. The laser types are *page printers*, meaning that it is necessary to store a complete page of information in the memory of the printer in order to print the page. Fonts for use with MS-DOS applications can be built-in, a few models in the past provided for adding fonts by way of a cartridge (surprisingly expensive), or, as is most usual for printing from Windows, the TrueType fonts will be used with the information sent to the printer by way of the driver.

- The manuals for laser printers often contain a lot of detail that is relevant only if you do **not** use Windows. You can ignore references to fonts and control codes if your printing is done from Windows.

When elaborate graphics are used this can require a large amount of memory, and some laser printers require 2 Mbyte or more of memory to function satisfactorily along with DTP programs. The quoted speed of most laser printers refers to repeated copies of a single page and does not refer to normal printing, which can be considerably slower. All quoted printing speeds for printers of any kind tend to be optimistic.

Laser printers work on a principle called Xerography (Trade Mark of the Xerox Corporation) which was invented in the 1960s. The similarities between the laser printer and the Xerox type of photocopier are so close that the manufacturers of laser printer are also manufacturers of copiers and the two products can be made in one assembly line. A page cannot be printed until the drum which is used to store the 'bit-image' of a page is fully 'printed' with electrical charges (the drum is usually printed more than once to form a page, but the printing does not start until all the print-bits are assembled in the memory). In addition, the mechanism depends on the paper being rolled continually over and against a drum, rather than being jerked in one-line steps as it is on other printer types. This makes the printer quieter in action than the dot-matrix type, and quieter even than some inkjet types.

The use of elaborate graphics calls for enough memory to store a full page. This does not mean that you cannot use a laser printer with only 512 Kbyte of memory — such a printer can cope perfectly well with ordinary pages of book printing that contain no graphics other than line drawings. It is also possible to handle more elaborate graphics if you confine the resolution to 150 dots per inch or lower.

In addition to memory, the laser printer also contains the components of a computer, with a main processor of its own. This processor is used to convert the pattern of bits in the memory into instructions for guiding the laser beam and turning the beam on or off so that the drum can be discharged in the correct places. This is how the laser printers can work with such a wide range of fonts and sizes and also with graphics.

• Note, however, that a laser printer cannot reproduce true shades of grey, because each dot that it prints is black. Gray shades can be simulated by mixing (dithering) black dots and white spaces, but this leads to a coarse appearance on a 300-dots per inch printer and is really satisfactory only on a typesetting grade of machine which works at 2400 dots per inch or more.

The laser printer uses a drum of synthetic material which is electrically charged (by an electrical discharge or corona through air which as a by-product produces ozone). Ozone is not good for you, it is a hazardous gas, and the laser printer should be used in a well-ventilated space. Any electrically charged object will attract small particles to it, and the purpose of charging the drum is to make it possible for finely-powdered ink (called toner) to be attracted to the charged points on the drum and to adhere.

The material of the drum, in addition to being a material which can be electrically charged, is also photoconductive, meaning that it becomes an electrical conductor when it is struck by light. When the drum becomes conductive, the electrical charge will leak away so that the drum can no longer attract or hold particles of toner. The principle of the printer is to make the drum conductive in selected parts, and this happens when the material is struck by a light beam. The laser beam is a beam of concentrated light that can be focused to a very small point, and it has the effect of making the material of the drum conductive where the beam strikes it. The beam intensity (on or off) and direction is controlled by the pattern of signals held in the memory of the printer, and this is why enough memory must be present to store information for a complete page.

- The light need not come from a laser, and copiers use a conventional light source, as do the (old) LCD-bar printers. The LED bar type uses light-emitting diodes which are similar to semiconducting lasers.

As the drum rotates, the laser beam, under the control of the built-in computer, is scanned across the drum. This scanning process uses the same principles (patented in 1886) as mechanical television used in the 1920s, with a revolving mirror or prism deflecting the beam. Once scanning is complete, the drum will contain on its surface an electrical voltage 'image' that corresponds exactly to the pattern that exists in the memory, corresponding to the pattern of black dots that will make up the image. Finely powdered resin, the toner, will now be coated over the drum and will stick to it only where the electric charge is large — at each black dot of the original page.

## Troubleshooting your PC printer

The coating process is done by using another roller, the *developing cylinder*, which is in contact with the toner powder, a form of dry ink. The toner is a light dry powder which is a non-conductor and also magnetic (some machines use a separate magnetic developer powder), and the developing cylinder is magnetised to ensure that it will be coated with toner as it revolves in contact with the toner from the cartridge. A scraper blade ensures that the coating is even. As the developing cylinder rolls close to the main drum, toner will be attracted across where the drum is electrically charged, relying on the electrical attraction being stronger than the magnetic attraction. Note that two forms of attraction, electrostatic and magnetic, are being used here.

Rolling a sheet of paper over the drum will now pass the toner to the paper, using another corona discharge to attract the toner particles to the paper by placing a positive charge on to the paper. After the toner has been transferred, the charge on the paper has to be neutralised to prevent the paper from remaining wrapped round the drum, and this is done by the static-eliminator blade.

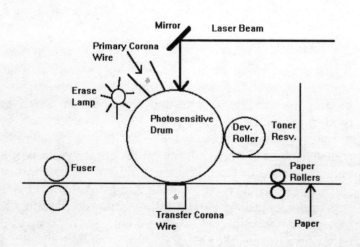

This leaves the toner only very faintly adhering to the paper, and it needs to be fixed permanently into place by passing the paper between hot rollers which melt the toner into the paper, giving the glossy appearance that is the mark of a good laser printer. The drum is then cleared of any residual toner by a sweeping blade, re-charged and made ready for the next page. The diagram shows the principles.

## Consumables

The main consumables of this process are the toner and the drum. The toner for most modern printers is contained in a replaceable cartridge, avoiding the need to decant this very fine powder from one container to another. The resin is comparatively harmless, but all fine powders are a risk to the lungs and also carry a risk of explosion. The drum on modern printers uses organic photoconductors (OPC) which are of low toxicity and which do not have to be returned to the manufacturers after replacement.

Drum replacement will, on average, be needed after each 10,000 to 80,000 copies. Some old models use a separate developer powder (a magnetic powder) in addition to toner, and the developer will have to be replenished at some time when the toner is also exhausted. The Hewlett-Packard LaserJet machines use a cartridge which contains both the photoconductive drum and the toner in one package, avoiding the need for separate renewal — the life is quoted for an average print density of word-processed text, but this figure will be drastically reduced if you print a lot of dense graphics and fonts. Typical life is 3,500 to 7,000 sides depending on the model you are using, but you can often obtain longer cartridge life if you print only text.

A typical ingredients list for toner appears as:

Styrene acrylate copolymer
Carbon black
Polypropylene

# Troubleshooting your PC printer

Charge control agent
Additives

of which the carbon black (or lampblack) is the finely
powdered carbon that is used in all printers ink. The styrene
acrylate is a plastics material similar to Perspex which is
finely ground, and has a low enough melting point to permit
the fusing action that melts the ink into the paper, binding
the carbon black so that it does not smudge. These are the
main active ingredients, and the others are concerned with
making the powder flow easily and ensuring that it will stick
to the drum and to the paper.

Some manufacturers arrange for cartridges that contain the
drum as well as the toner to be recycled. This is well
organised in the USA, but it is not so simple in the UK, and
you may experience difficulties if you want to dispose of
cartridges in a responsible way. A few Charity shops will
collect cartridges for recycling, and there are often
advertisements for recycling in the computer magazines.
You should not dispose of a toner cartridge in a dustbin.

## Light sources

The normal type of laser printer uses the laser beam and
rotating mirror or prism arrangement, but there are some
types of printers which are classed as laser printers but
which do not use a laser beam. These are LED-bar or LCD-
mask types which use the same principles of light beams
affecting a charged drum, but without the use of a laser
beam scanning over the drum. Instead, a line matrix of
miniature light sources is used.

These types are not page printers, and they can work line by
line, so requiring very little memory. They were originally
intended as replacements for daisywheel and dot-matrix
printers for word-processing applications rather than as a
competitor for the DTP type of laser printer, but several have
now been developed into high-resolution printers in their

own right. A notable modern example is the remarkably small and light Oki 4W.

On such a machine, the LED array is located in the lid and can easily be wiped clean each time a cartridge is renewed. The drum can be seen when the lid is open, and with the lid closed the LED array is close to the surface of the drum, with light-shields around it. Because opening the lid exposes the drum to light, you should never do this when the printer is in a bright light (such as full sunlight).

## Memory

The traditional type of laser print usually comes nowadays with 1 Mbyte or more of memory, and for most purposes no additional memory is needed. If you do need additional memory (indicated by printing that extends only over a part of each page) then it is very expensive compared to the normal EDO RAM that is used in your computer. This has led to the development of Windows or GDI printers, in which the main memory of your computer is used rather than using memory in the laser printer itself. This makes the printing action rather slower, but makes the printer cheaper.

• You need, of course, to have adequate memory in your computer, and a typical minimum for working with one of these printers and Windows is 32 Mbyte. Be careful if you are offered an old printer of this type, because some of them did not work with Windows 95, only with Windows 3.1.

The LED type of printer needs only a one-line buffer memory, because the bar of lights is controlled like the line of pins in the old-style comb-needle matrix printers.

## Consumables

Paper is the most consumed item, and laser printers use, as you might expect, the photocopier grade of paper whose cost is very low compared to that of specialised inkjet paper or the continuous paper preferred by dot-matrix machines

Good quality copier paper should consist of fibres which are all aligned along the longer axis of the paper, making the paper behave more uniformly when subject to electric charges (and discharges). It also allows the paper to feed through the machine with less tendency to curl. In addition, since the toner is fixed to the paper by fairly intense heating, the paper must not darken or curl when it is heated. These requirements make the paper more expensive to produce, though some shopping around can sometimes reveal better prices than can be obtained from local suppliers. Try Staples if you have one locally.

Whatever is claimed by manufacturers, the use of very heavy (more than 90 grams per square metre) and expensively finished paper is not justifiable. Such paper will often feed badly, forming ridges, and will allow toner to smear. Very heavy paper will stick in the printer or cause loud protests from the rollers. Lighter and more absorbent papers usually produce better results — try cheap grades first and always try a sample before you buy several hundred packs.

The other major costs are replacement of toner and of the print drum. Toner is a fine powder which must not be allowed to spill into the atmosphere, and the print drum is constructed using a photosensitive material which must not be handled or unduly exposed to light.

Some manufacturers have made the replacement of both toner and drum particularly easy for the user, for other (usually older and fast office types) the task is far from easy and better done by a maintenance mechanic. Maintenance does not simply cover the replacement of the toner and drum, it also concerns cleaning. Because of the way that electric charges attract all small particles, laser printers tend to become clogged up with fine dust, composed of stray toner and house dust in almost equal measure. Dust is, as always, an enemy of mechanical parts, so that cleaning and lubrication schedules are of considerable importance. A vacuum cleaner can be used to take dust from the inside of the printer, but it will spray out the toner from its bag unless you are using a cleaner that can cope with very fine dust.

## Paper paths

The paper path in a laser printer is often much more convoluted than the path of the typical dot-matrix or inkjet type. This is because so many processes are involved, so that the paper cannot be left to be moved against just one roller. This type of path makes it impossible to print on thicker material on the laser printers currently sold for small-business or home use, though more recent designs can be obtained with a straighter path.

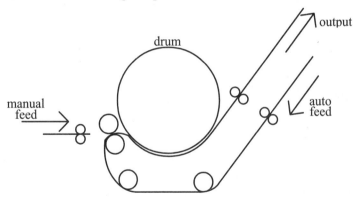

In addition, the paper is heated to around 200°C to fix the toner, and this imposes some restrictions on anything other than plain paper. Self-sealing envelopes, for example, are usually ruled out for use with any laser printer, and any self-adhesive labels that you buy must be certified for laser printer use. Envelopes with clear panels are also unlikely to survive the heating action and can leave sticky deposits inside the printer, but the nature of these envelopes means that you would not normally print on to them. Use laser

# Troubleshooting your PC printer

labels on any stationery that you cannot pass through the printer, and remember that elaborate printed colour logos and headings may also melt in the laser printer.

## Speed

The quoted speed of a laser printer can range from a leisurely 3–4 pages per minute to 24 pages per minute (or more) for the fastest office types, and the faster the printer the higher the price — typically £1,700 for the fastest monochrome varieties. For many purposes, a very high speed is unimportant, and it can be a positive handicap if the printer does not have a good output tray arrangement.

A slow printer can be left with a tray full of paper and with Windows background printing set up, can be allowed to churn away until the paper is finished while you use the computer for other purposes. If the printer is one of the types that spews out the printed sheets over the top and can allow them to fall back into the input tray then you have to keep a much closer eye on it, and this can be very awkward.

## Colour

Colour printing with laser printers is possible, using three cartridges with the usual yellow, cyan and magenta toners. Starting prices are in the £3,000 to £4,000 region, and printing is slow because of the need to print and register three sets of image dots.

Because of the usual limitations of printing in dots, colours have to be simulated by dithering as on inkjet colour printers, but the melting of the dots leads to a better colour appearance, all without the need to use special paper. You can get a good impression of the print quality that can be achieved if you get some colour photographs copied in a colour copier at your local print shop.

## Cartridges

Many of the laser printers currently available use comparatively cheap cartridges of toner, some around the size of a tube of toothpaste. These are usually good for 1,000 to 2,000 sides of A4, and the larger types can cope with more. On such machines, the drum will have to be replaced at intervals, and these intervals can vary enormously, anything from 10,000 sides to almost 100,000 sides.

Hewlett-Packard, by contrast, have always used a cartridge that contains all the items in one package, so that when you replace a cartridge you are replacing the drum as well as the toner and the other parts such as corona wires and scraper blades. This certainly cuts down on servicing costs, and the price that you pay for this convenience is a more costly cartridge.

## Controls

Some laser printers of a more traditional design have a control panel that allows you to specify items such as paper size, default font, character set and so on. These had to be used in the days when printing was done from MS-DOS applications, but when Windows is used as the operating system these choices are not needed, so that the modern trend is to provide only a few controls (such as on/off line) or even none at all.

This allows the machine to be totally controlled by software, and usually requires the use of a bi-directional printer cable so that the printer can signal items such as *paper jam* or *toner low* back to the software to be displayed as a warning on the screen.

## PostScript

At one time, a laser printer suitable for Desk Top Publishing (DTP) use would use a software print control system called PostScript, a trademark of the Adobe Corporation.

## Troubleshooting your PC printer

PostScript is a system of coding how print looks (and also graphics) using ordinary text characters, and its most noticeable characteristic is that it generates huge files. For example, a book chapter that uses about 50 Kbyte of memory in its word processor format can need as much as 3 Mbyte in PostScript form.

With the use of TrueType fonts in PC computers and the ability of word processors such as Word, WordPro and WordPerfect to handle graphics as well as text, the use of PostScript on smaller laser printers has died out. The system is still used on large laser printers and on typesetting printers, however, such as the Agfa and the Linotronic machines, because it is independent of the type of software used to produce it. In other words, if you send a document to a printing firm using a PostScript file, it does not matter which word processor you used to produce the document, and the printing firm does not need to possess a copy of that word processor. The development of drives that write CD ROM discs makes it easier to send PostScript files around the country without using large numbers of floppies.

### Laser choice

Most of the lower-cost laser printers use as their standard the Hewlett-Packard LaserJet, and they emulate the codes used by that printer (which is itself not expensive in its *home user* forms). This type of printer is excellent for word-processing and graphics, and virtually all word-processing and graphics software will provide printer driver software for the H-P printer. The most recent Series 6 LaserJets are excellent machines which are produced in a range of prices for small and large users alike. Older models are still a good buy because these printers have a long life and supply of toner is as certain as anything in computing can be.

There are laser printers from every firm that ever manufactured dot-matrix printers, most of the firms that manufacture copiers, and a few more besides, and the choice is enormous, though you need to remember that the number of different print engines is limited.

## Using the laser printer

The working heart of the laser printer is known as the *engine* and there are only a few basic engines (such as the Canon) used in all of the laser printers that are currently manufactured. This makes it all the more surprising that there is not more interchangeability between makes for such items as font cartridges, toner cartridges, replacement drums and so on. If you are buying a laser printer for the first time, it pays to enquire on the costs of these consumable items, because these costs are often much more important than the cost of the printer itself.

You should also examine the paper path and handling, because a small footprint is not a great advantage if you have to stand next to the printer to prevent printed sheets from mixing with the blank paper.

# 9 Laser printer problems

Many problems that arise with a laser printer can be solved simply by some cleaning followed by changing the cartridge, and this is particularly true of the H-P types. Toner dust is the main source of problems in machines that use a separate toner cartridge, because the seal between the toner cartridge and the drum cartridge is not always satisfactory, allowing toner to spray around the machine. If any of this toner reaches the revolving mirror/prism assembly of a conventional laser printer it can be wiped off only after some considerable dismantling.

- Unless you have attended a manufacturer's printer maintenance course, you should not attempt to dig inside the optical system of a laser printer. You must never open a laser printer that is operating. You should take precautions, such as wearing a mask, if you are working with exposed toner, and you should not try to refill toner cartridges in an unventilated space.

Note that many of the LED printer types have the LED matrix fitted to the opening lid, and you are expected to wipe this array each time you replace a toner cartridge. This type of printer does not present the hazards that are present in the laser-beam type.

- For all laser-printer faults, the easiest response to any fault is to replace the drum cartridge, If the problem disappears, it has originated in a part of the cartridge. You should always keep a spare cartridge (or cartridges if your machine uses separate toner and drum cartridges).

## Staining

A fault that is fairly common is that the paper has stained edges — this is also a familiar fault of photocopiers. The cause is that toner has leaked on to one of the rollers, and it appears at the edges because there is always a sheet of paper over the main part of the roller while the printer is working.

It is usually easy to clip out the roller, and it can be cleaned using soap and *cold* water. It is important to use cold water, because hot water can melt the toner and secure it in place. Washing is quite useless, however, if the leakage continues, and if the printer is a LaserJet the simple remedy is to remove the cartridge, clean the inside of the printer and then install a new cartridge.

For other printers, after cleaning the main roller you should examine other rollers, and clean the inside of the printer thoroughly. You may need to change the drum cartridge if the toner leak comes from there, because the leak may be due to a poor seal between the drum cartridge and the toner cartridge, and this is something that is not easy to remedy, particularly when you have a nearly-full toner cartridge in use.

## Streaking/shading

Background shading sometimes appears, particularly when you are printing envelopes or labels. This can often be avoided if the printer controls allow you to alter the amount of electric charge — this may be labelled as the *print density* control. Another cause of background shading is dust on the lenses and mirrors of a conventional laser printer, and you should send the printer to have the optics cleaned and checked. You can clean the LED array for yourself if you use the LED-bar type of printer.

*White areas* on a printed page are usually due to damp paper. Allow the paper to dry, and meantime replace it with a fresh supply from an unopened pack that has been stored in dry conditions.

*Vertical white streaks* are fairly unusual and usually indicate the need to clean the charge corona wire in the cartridge. For H-P or similar models, simply change the cartridge. Some other models provide a cleaning tool. If in doubt, change the drum assembly complete with corona wire.

*Grey shading* around the print can be caused by a variety of causes. Try a different batch of paper to start with. If this has no effect, check that the printer has no obvious toner leaks or other dust. Vacuum-clean the printer if you have a suitable cleaner that will retain toner, and try some test prints. The next thing to check is the darkness setting. Try printing with a darker setting and then with a lighter setting, and use the setting that causes the problems to disappear. Try another cartridge if none of these remedies has any effect.

The other causes of grey shading are more serious and you should not try to sort them out for yourself unless you have experience in dismantling laser optical systems. The contact between the high voltage connector earthing spring and the cartridge may need to be cleaned. The mirror in the optical system (or the LED line in this type of printer) may be dirty. The fixing assembly may need to be renewed.

A *white vertical line* often indicates that you are running out of toner. As a check, take out the toner cartridge and rock it from side to side ten times, then replace it. If this results in some perfect printing, it's going to be time to renew the toner very soon, probably within 50 pages.

Other possible causes, which need expert attention, are a dirty mirror or fixing assembly.

A more unusual problem is a *grey vertical line or lines*, and this can be caused by poor quality (or damp) paper. Try also a different cartridge. Other possibilities are to try different (lighter/darker) settings for the darkness adjustment, or to replace the fixing assembly (not a DIY job).

*Random variations in shading* may also be due to toner running out or to poor paper quality (or dampness). The darkness control may also need some adjustment. A dirty mirror or corona wire can also be the cause, as is a dirty high voltage connector, fixing assembly, or transfer roller.

*Pale print overall* can also be a paper fault, mirror, darkness adjustment, high voltage connector, transfer roller

A *grey horizontal line* can be attributed to paper faults, dirty or damaged pick-up rollers, and other possible causes are the restoration unit and the fixing assembly

A *black vertical line* almost indicates a fault in the cartridge, such as a dirty corona wire or fixing assembly.

A *white horizontal line* can be attributed to paper, but it can also be caused by overloading the paper tray or cassette, so that the paper wrinkles as it is fed in. If this fails, try a new cartridge

## Dithering

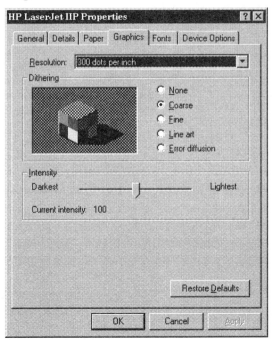

# Troubleshooting your PC printer

A common cause of problems with graphics printing is the dithering setting. The printer driver will always contain a pane that offers various dithering options, and these are not always well explained.

The illustration shows the dithering settings for the H-P IIP printer, and the advice is that the coarse setting should be used for graphics that use shading. The usual advice is that the dithering setting should be the reverse of the printer resolution, so that coarse dithering is used for high-resolution printers. On some later machines the advice is usually to try different settings until you find the ones that provide the quality that you want. You may find that the line-art setting is the most useful if most of your graphics are of this type.

## Paper curling

Paper curling almost always indicates that the paper is unsuitable or that you are using the wrong side of the paper. This is a very common problem if you want to print on both sides of your paper, and you should try to avoid this. If you must use both sides, buy suitable paper, set your word processor to print odd numbered pages only, and allow the sheets to cool, then keep flattened under a press overnight. The next day, set your word processor to print the even-numbered pages, and if possible, feed in the pages one by one because they will probably jam in the automatic feed.

- Remember that if you are printing on the blank side of paper that has come from a copier you should not expect the best possible results because you are working on the wrong side of the paper, and it has already been through a laser-printing type of process.

## Jamming

Jamming is unusual if the paper is of reasonable quality unless you are trying to print on the other side of printed paper. On some printers, you are instructed to fan out a bundle of paper, restore it to a bundle, and then insert and press the *Form Feed* control (if there is one). Several printer instruction manuals also warn you not to add more paper to an existing stack, and the preferred method is to remove the existing paper, add more, and follow the method described for new paper.

- Never use paper that is sticky (because it had a label attached) or which still has labels in place. Make certain that any label sheets that you use are certified fit for use with a laser printer. Do not try to print on self-sealing envelopes.

### Roller and feed problems

A grumbling noise while paper is being printed is quite common and not serious. It is usually caused by worn rollers or dry bearings, and on an H-P machine it will probably disappear when you renew a cartridge. On other machines, it is usually a simple task to clip out the rollers and insert new ones, or to lubricate roller bearing if this is permitted.

If paper feeds incorrectly at times, try cleaning the paper pickup roller with isopropanol (such as spectacle lens cleaning liquid). If you find two or more sheets feeding at once, get into the habit of fanning the paper out to unstick the sheets before you insert the paper into the input tray.

### Sundry points

Lubrication is not usually a DIY task, and where it is advised it always uses silicone oils — mineral oils are totally forbidden on the plastics which are almost universally used for bearings on light machinery.

Users are often advised to start a new run of a major printing with a fresh toner supply. Though it is inadvisable to start a run when the toner is almost finished, replenishing toner is not advisable before a major piece of work. When toner has been replenished, the first set of pages may be over-inked and badly smudged.

Following toner replenishment, always make some test copies onto absorbent paper until you are sure that the toner is flowing correctly. I have never experienced these problems with the LaserJet machine.

Note that toner cannot be vacuum-cleaned effectively — it is too fine to be retained in the bag of the cleaner unless you are using a Medivac (TM) or Nilfisk (TM) type of machine. If you get toner on clothes, brush or wipe off. If you have to wash the clothes, use cold water. Avoid hot water at all costs because it can melt the toner into the fabric, making it impossible to remove.

The laser printer is not the universal answer to printing requirements, because though the cost of buying a laser printer has dropped dramatically since the early days, the price of maintaining such a printer is still high. The consumables are costly, particularly toner (powdered ink), and when more extensive servicing is required the chemicals that are involved are toxic and expensive. Laser printers, incidentally, should, like photocopiers, be used only in a well-ventilated space.

## Recycled laser cartridges

The high price of replacement cartridges makes the use of recycled or refilled cartridges tempting, but you should approach this with care. There should be no problem in buying compatible or recycled *toner* cartridges, and even if you buy new cartridges from the manufacturer you may notice that the label indicates that recycled material has been used.

Buying a recycled cartridge of the type that contains the drum and other parts is quite another matter. In seven years of using a H-P LaserJet, I never had a recycled cartridge from any source that was satisfactory, though compatible cartridges from reputable sources such as Verbatim caused no problems. The generally poor quality of recycled cartridges (one was cracked and leaking toner) led me to the habit of destroying used cartridges so that there was no chance of them being used again.

If you want to consider recycled cartridges, you will have noted the manufacturer's comments. In the USA, a manufacturer is not allowed to use this as an excuse for failing to honour a guarantee, but the UK is more lax in this respect. It does not cost much to wait until the guarantee has expired. Once again, you may find that a 'new' cartridge contains recycled parts in any case.

Laser cartridges are a high-profit item (like razor-blades), and manufacturers and resellers prefer to keep the prices high. If the proposed EEC recommendations on the garage trade go through, it may become illegal to service any machines with parts that do not come from the original manufacturers. This will in all likelihood lead to very sharp increases in prices.

Some types of toner cartridges are quite easy to refill, and it is a temptation to put in a pound's worth of toner powder rather than pay £15 or do for someone else to do it. This all hinges on whether you can get toner at bulk prices, and if you are happy at handling the material. Personally, I would not, though I am perfectly happy to replenish an ink-jet cartridge or re-ink a dot-matrix printer ribbon.

# Appendix A

## Table of equivalents for inkjet cartridges

Your inkjet printer will specify a cartridge type which is often that of the (badged) manufacturer. In fact, most inkjet printers can use one of a smaller number of cartridges made by the manufacturer of the printing engine. Some of these are listed below, concentrating on inkjet printers that are available in the UK, and ignoring specialised printers and some that are seldom seen here.

Note that most of the cartridges listed here are originally manufactured by Canon (CAN), Hewlett-Packard (HP) or Epson (EPS). The initials CMY refer to use of coloured inks Cyan, Magenta and Yellow.

| Manufr. | Models | Part No. |
|---|---|---|
| Apple | APLM 6901/02/03/04 | CANBJI-643/C/M/Y |
| | Stylewriter 2400 | CANBCI-21/BC20 |
| | Color Stylewriter Pro | CANBJI-201-/C/M/Y |
| | Portable Stylewriter APL, Stylewriter APL | M8052G/A; CANBC-01 |
| | Stylewriter I APL, Stylewriter II APL | M8041G/A; CANBC-02 |
| Brother | HJ-100, HJ-100I, HJ-400, Whisperwriter WP7000J | BROIN-10; CANBC-01 |
| | HJ-770 | BROIN-20; CANBJI-642 |

| Canon | BJ-5, BJ-10,<br>BJ-10E, BJ-10EX,<br>BJ-10sx, BJ-10V,<br>BJ-20, BJ-30,<br>BX-200,<br>Starwriter60,<br>Starwriter70,<br>Starwriter80,<br>Starwriter80Deluxe,<br>Starwriter85,<br>Starwriter95,<br>VP500 | CANBC-01 |
|---|---|---|
| | BJ-200, BJ-200e,<br>BJ-200ex, BJ-220JC,<br>BJ-220JS, BJ-230 | CANBC-02 |
| | BJ-300, BJ-330 | CANBJI-642 |
| | BJC-210/240<br>BJC-600<br>BJC-800, BJC-820,<br>BJC-880, BJC-880J,<br>BJP-C80, CJP-C80 | CANBC-02/05<br>CANBJI-201/C/M/Y<br><br>CANBJI-643/C/M/Y |
| | BJC-4000/4200/4550<br>BN22 Compri,<br>BN32P Compri,<br>BN100C Compri | CANBCI-20/21<br><br>CANBJ-101 |
| | BP10D, BP12D,<br>BP25D, BP26D,<br>BP35D, BP36D,<br>BP1025D, BP1211D,<br>BP1225D, BP1425D,<br>BP1445D. BP5020D,<br>BP5220D. BP5420D | CANCJ3A; HP51604A |

## Troubleshooting your PC printer

| | | |
|---|---|---|
| Canon | CLC10, Notejet486, P670 | CANBC40 CANBJ-101 CANBJI-642 |
| Citizen | Projet, ProjetII | HP51626/51608A |
| Diconix | 150, 150PLUS, 180si, 300, 300W, M150PLUS | DIC8223893; HP51604A |
| Epson | Stylus 300 | EPS SO20031; CANBC-01 |
| | Stylus 400, Stylus 800, Stylus 800+, Stylus 1000 | EPS SO20025 |
| | Stylus Color Stylus Color II/IIs Stylus Color 400/600/800 | EPS SO20034/36 EPS SO20047/49 EPS S020093/SO20108 |
| Facit | J1200, J1250 | HP51604A |
| Fujitsu | Breeze100, Breeze100PLUS, Breeze200, DEX530 | HP51625A/51608A |
| Hewlett-Packard | 1200/1600C | HP51640A/C/M/Y |
| | 2225A, 2225B, 2225C, 2225C, 2225D, 2225 Thinkjet 2227A, 2227A QuietJetPlus, 2228A QuietJet | HP51604A |

| Hewlett-Packard | 2276A, 2277A, Designjet 200, Deskjet, Deskjet Plus, Deskjet 400/500, Deskjet 500C, Deskjet 510, Deskjet 520, Deskjet 550C, Deskjet 560C, Deskwriter, Deskwriter C, Deskwriter 510, Deskwriter 520, Deskwriter 550C, Deskwriter 560C | HP51626A/51608A |
| --- | --- | --- |
| | Designjet 650C | HP51640A |
| | Deskjet Portable, Deskjet 300J, Deskjet 310 | HP51633A |
| | Deskjet 600/60/90C | HP51629A/51649A |
| | Deskjet 820/50/70C | HP51645A/51641A |
| | Deskjet 1200C/P/S | HP51640A/C/M/Y |
| | Deskwriter 310 | HP51633A/51625A |
| | PaintJet | HP51606C/51606A |
| | PaintJet XL-Black | HP51606A |
| | PaintJet XL300 | HP51639A/C/M/Y |
| | Paintwriter | HP51606C/51606A |
| | Paintwriter XL-Black | HP51606A |
| | QuietJet, QuietJet Plus, ThinkJet | HP51604A |
| IBM | 4070IJ Model 1, 4070IJ Model 2 | IBM1380630; CANBC-01 |

## Troubleshooting your PC printer

| | | |
|---|---|---|
| IBM | 4072 Execjet | IBM1380479; CANBJI-64 |
| | 4079 Color Jetprinter | IBM13080490/91/92/93; CANBJI-643/C/M/Y |
| Integrex | Betajet | HP51626A/51608A |
| | Colourjet 2 | HP51626A/51625A |
| Lexmark | 4076/2070/1020 | 1382060/1380619/20 |
| Mannes-mann Tally | MT93, MT94 | CANBJI-642 |
| | T7018, T7040 | HP51626A/51608A /51625A |
| NEC | Jetmate 400, Jetmate 800 | HP51626A/51608A |
| Nixdorf | MD-16, MD-22 | HP51604A |
| Oki | 2010 | 1380619/20 |
| Olivetti | JP150, JP150W, JP250, JP350, JP350W,OFX 2035, OFX 2045, OFX 2100, OFX 3100 | HP51626A/51608A |
| | JP360, JP450 | HP51626A/51625A |
| Olympia | Colorstar | HP51606C/51608A |
| | OF 710, OF 720, Quietstar 4 | HP51626A/51608A |
| Seikosha | Speedjet 200 | HP51626A/51608A |
| Sharp | FO-1700, FO-3700, UX01200, UX-1500 | SHPFO-40CG; HP51626A |
| Siemens | 4812-L10 | HP51626A/51608A |
| Smith Corona | Coronajet 200J | HP51626A/51608A |
| Star Micronics | Starjet SJ-48, Starjet SJ-48Plus | CANBC-01 |

| Triumph-Adler | JPR630, JPR635, JPR7825, JPR7825WS, JPR7840, JPR7850, JPR7850WS | HP51626A/51608A |
|---|---|---|
| | JPR7845, JPR7860 | HP51626A/51625A |

# Appendix B

Net sites for some printer manufacturers. These were correct at the time of writing but may be changed without notice.

**Agfa**

http://www.agfa.com

**Brother**

http://www.brother.com/eu-printer/index.html

**Canon(Europe)**

http://www.europe.canon.com/

**Canon(UK)**

http://www.canon.co.uk/

**Canon(USA)**

http://www.canon.com/

**Citizen**

http://www.citizen-printer.co.uk/users/jg19

**Epson**

http://www.epson.com/connects/index.html

**Hewlett-Packard**

http://www.hp.com

http://hpcc998.external.hp.com

**IBM(Europe)**

http://www.europe.ibm.com

**IBM(USA)**

http://www.pc.ibm.com

**Kyocera(USA)**

> http://www.kyocera.com/

**Kyocera(UK)**

> http://www.kyocera.co.uk

**Lexmark**

> http://www.lexmark.com/

**Minolta**

> http://www.minolta.co.uk

**Oki**

> http://www.okidata.com

**Olivetti**

> http://www.olivetti.com

**Panasonic**

> http://www.panasonic.com

**Panasonic UK**

> http://www.panasonic.co.uk/

**Tally**

> http://www.tally.com

**Windows 95 drivers**

> http://www.cobb.com/w95/software/drivers.htm

**Xerox**

> http://www.xerox.com/

# Appendix C

Some telephone help-lines for printer manufacturers are noted below. These were correct at the time of writing, but may have changed since.

Brother.............................(01613) 306531

Canon..............................(0990) 143743

Epson .............................(0144) 261144

H–P.................................(0171) 5125202

Kyocera ..........................(01606) 867015

Minolta ...........................(01908) 200400

Oki..................................(02753) 819800

Panasonic........................(01344) 583508

# INDEX

## Troubleshooting your PC printer

## Troubleshooting your PC printer

# Troubleshooting your PC printer